THE BOOK OF SOUL RETRIEVAL
HOW TO USE MAGICK TO HEAL YOUR SOUL

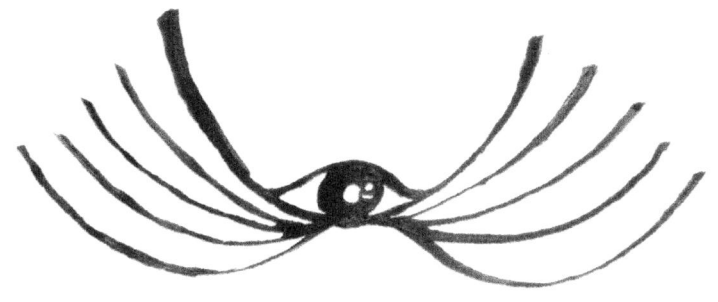

ENOCH B. PETRUCELLY
WITH
SARA PETRUCELLY

THE BOOK OF SOUL RETRIEVAL

HOW TO USE MAGICK TO HEAL YOUR SOUL

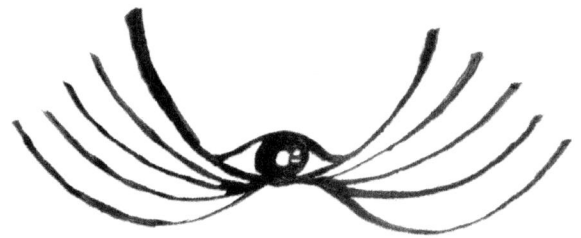

Rights Reserved
© 2018 By Enoch B. Petrucelly
Second Edition
All artwork, sigils (with the exception of the Sigil of Rameel), cover art and design are creations of the author of this book.

Printed By CreateSpace, an Amazon.com Company

Contents

Introduction 6
How to Use this Book 7
Chapter 1-Energy Management 8
Chapter 2-Gratitude For Life 31
Chapter 3-Enemies 35
Chapter 4-Embodiment 48
Chapter 5-Magickal Practice Basics 53
Magickal Practice Basics Part One Ritual tools 54
Simple Clearing Rite 55
Basic Ritual Tools In Order Of Importance 56
The Rite Of Consecration 65
Chapter 6-Magickal Practice Basics Part Two 67
The Cleansing Rite Of The Goddess 69
The Circle of Heka (Magick) 72
Chapter 7-Advanced Preliminary Rites of Soul Retrieval 74
The use of your blood in Magick 75
The Use of Baneful or Cursing Magick 77
The Curse Breaker Rite 79
The Curse Breaker Rite step by step 82
The Rite Of Sovereignty 85
The Rite of Sovereignty step by step 88
The Rite Of Implant Removal 91
Sara Petrucelly On Chakra Removal 92
The Rite Of Chakra Removal step by step 98
Implant Removal Meditation 101
Implant Removal Meditation step by step 101
Chapter 8-The Rite of Protection 104

The Rite of Protection step by step.................................106

Chapter 9-The Rite of Soul Retrieval...................................109

Rite Of Soul Retrieval step by step......................................112

Chapter 10-The True Face of The Moon 115

The Rite Of Destroying The Artificial Moon's Influence Over You..119

The Rite of Destroying The Artificial Moon's Influence Over You step by step..124

Chapter 11-The True Face of Nibiru Exposed 127

The Rite Of Cursing Nibiru And Destroying It's Influence Over You..128

The Rite Of Cursing Nibiru And Destroying It's Influence Over You step by step..132

Chapter 12-Frequency Control On The Grid 135

The Rite Of Destroying Death Tower Control 137

The Rite Of Destroying Death Tower Control step by step..141

Chapter 13-What Comes Next? 144

Afterword 146

Acknowledgments

I express much gratitude as always to my spirit guide Mike for his unwavering support and advice in my Left Hand Path journey, to those Neteru who have been dedicated to this important work of soul retrieval (Ra, Horus, Set, Nehebkau, Ammit, Ptah, and Seker). I am also grateful to Rameel for agreeing to participate in The Protection Rite in this book. I am very grateful to my sister Sara for her friendship and willingness to put the Rites in this book to the test. To all my friends and family who support me despite my somewhat odd spiritual views, thank you all. And lastly I want to thank Lucifer for his powerful knowledge and gnosis that has made the revisions of this Second Edition of The Book Of Soul Retrieval possible.

Introduction

This Little book of Magick and healing is a tome which I as a young, Male Witch wish I had when I was just starting out. It was written for those who wish to strengthen their conscious connection to their immortal, timeless Inter-Dimensional-Selves. It was written so those who pick it up will be empowered with the knowledge of themselves, of what they truly want to do with their lives, and how to be healed in ways that they never believed could be done.

Expect life changing events that will alter your mind, body and soul for the better should you pick up this book and do what it says with sincerity. You are at the core a powerful being that is not a slave to spiritual or man-made forces. This fact will be impressed upon you if you decide to move forward into this gnosis. The book consist of specific rites designed to bring you into a state of embodiment that is nothing short of the ultimate realization of what it is you want and need to do in your life.

Once the process of Soul Healing is begun, you will quickly realize some basic principles of being that you have no doubt heard before, yet never really integrated for lack of knowing how exactly to do so. This book is an initiator into this path of re-integrating lost or forgotten pieces of your Self.

This revised edition of The Book of Soul Retrieval contains Words of Power that are used to enhance and dramatically amplify the evokations of the Spirits who will help you in the Rites found within this book. It also contains a new, powerful Rite of Protection, which calls upon the Watcher Rameel for his energies of psychic defense. May you have great success and empowerment in your journey!

Enoch B. Petrucelly
LHP Male Witch
April 27th, 2018

How to Use this Book

This book is designed to be worked through from beginning to end in a systematic and step by step way. You may find that certain steps or chapters do not apply to you because you have already done/learned them in your own way. If this is the case, skip the specific chapter or steps which you feel are not needed.

You may feel drawn to certain techniques or rites more than others. If you are drawn to a certain rite within this book, I do recommend that you go over the preliminary chapters about the hows and whys of Magickal Practice itself first before moving into the practice of Magick. It is necessary to have an elementary understanding of how Magick works before performing it. It is also very important to understand the principals of Energy Management before moving into Magickal Practice. Please do not perform Rites that you know you are not ready to do. Take it step by step for best results and to get the most out of this book.

Chapter 1
Energy Management

Energy Management is important for anyone in this modern world, especially those who are drawn to the path of Magickal Practice. Practicing spirituality or Magick of any kind without the discipline and understanding of how energy works within the body and outside of the body can be dangerous and may ultimately lead to psychological and emotional problems that are not easily fixed. It is best to at least learn basics of how to take care of one's energy before beginning to practice Magick.

The issues created by lack of understanding how energy works cannot be solved by medication nor therapy alone. They can only be helped and healed by the knowledge of proper energy work itself. Yes, therapy or talking out problems is helpful and necessary for many, but it is limited and will not solve the problem a person is having if the roots of their issues are energy related. And everything is energy and thus most emotional or psychological issues that are given a label are connected to a person's energy body. Do not misunderstand, I do believe in medication and therapy for healing and health within reason. I am simply pointing out that spiritual health, is just as, if not much more important than taking pills and getting therapy. It is a very important part of overall health that can no longer be ignored by health professionals. It must be included in a person's life if they are to be happy and healthy. Without it there will always be something missing and an imbalance will usually manifest.

Energy Management is a tool for heath and even protection from psychic attack. I am not only talking about other embodied individuals, but even more so making you aware of the controlling energies of the world we live in that feed on us without our even noticing. If you have no protection or awareness of your vital energies, then it will be quite easy for some parasitic entity to drain you even while you are wide awake and aware. You are a sitting duck without understanding the basics of your own vital energies.

I personally had to learn these details of spiritual practice the hard way. I did not know that I would be knocked on my face over and over again until I got it right. I am handing you the keys to grow and protect yourself that I had to suffer trial and error to obtain. These Energy Management keys and the Rites found within this book may enable you to break the energy draining cycle that inflicts so many of us.

Energy Management is also the ability to maintain a good and positive amount of Chi in your body at all times. This requires daily maintenance and awareness. You must never blow out your energy to the point where you become vulnerable to outside energies that wish to harm or draw your vital energies out of you.

There are many things we do every day that attribute to energy expenditure. As with money you should never spend more than what you have, unless absolutely necessary. If you have an abundance of money and you use it correctly, it will increase to greater amounts. The same principle applies to managing your body's vital energies or Chi. If you have an abundance of Chi energy it will create greater amounts of Chi on its own; unless you fail to protect it, you expend too much at once, you use it in a way that is out of alignment with your Inter-Dimensional-Self, or if you use more than you are creating/accumulating day by day. I will go into more detail in the next section.

Energy Management From "A" To "Z"

A. Grounding

- What is grounding?

Grounding is the process of connecting yourself and your energy with the energy of the Earth Plane herself. It is the first and most important thing you can do to stay energetically healthy. It is an anchor that allows clarity and centeredness in your daily life.

- Why should I ground myself?

Because it will automatically clear out your energy/subtle bodies of stuck garbage and attachments that have clung to you during your days. It balances your energies automatically if you do it correctly. It also charges your energy system so that you can feel your best mentally/spiritually throughout your day. It allows one to feel centered and focused. Less scattered and rattled by daily life. It may help you feel calm and present in the moment with less anxiety.

- How often should I ground myself?

Every morning for sure and if you have had a particularly challenging day, before bed as well.

- How do I ground myself/how does it work?

First get comfortable and relax. You may ground standing up or seated, but do not slouch if you can help it. Take deep, slow breaths through your nose preferably. Then follow the steps of visualization. If you cannot visualize then use your sense of feeling. Eyes closed unless you are able to do the visualization with them open and place hands on your knees if you are seated, down at your sides if you are standing.

Step One:
See the Lower Dan-tien (we will call it), just below the navel, deep in your abdomen in front of the spine. It often appears as a red ball of light/energy, but if you can see it in your mind's eye do not try to alter it's appearance or color. Connect with this center and feel the heat coming from it. Place your right hand on it as you breath and connect.

Step Two:
See a cord of bright energy…like a fiber optic cable connected to the Dan-tien extending downward to an olive green round center at you feet (between them). This circular ball of energy or Earth Star is usually a shade of green, but once again do not change its appearance if you see it in your mind's eye.

Step Three:
See the olive green center extend downward into the earth below you feet. Allow it to descend slowly at first then start to pick up speed as it drops deeper and deeper into the Earth. Send the Earth Star center into the deep layers of the Earth until you feel energy begin to rise up your legs and torso.

Step Four:
Once you will feel the vibrant, gentle, dark, and creative energies of Mother Earth. Take a minute to synchronize with this energy and see roots growing out from your Earth Star into the surrounding abundant Yin Chi. This will automatically balance your own body's energy. Thank the Earth now for allowing you to synchronize with her.

Step Five:
Now take a few minutes to communicate your needs to the Earth. Remember she is a conscious being. You do not need to use words, just communicate your feelings. Do not forget to send the feelings of gratitude to her for her help. If you need to name her, then my suggestion is to use the name "Naamah" or some would say "Gaia" as well. Both are names of the Mother Goddess or Earth Goddesses that are very primal, powerful and at the same time, loving. If you need extra energy to get

through your day then ask her for it. Ask her to "charge your energy system". Any other pressing matters that you may be worrying about can be released to her as well. You may also ask her to clear your energy system of harmful, stuck energies. Once you feel centered, balanced and well, open your eyes and begin your day.

B. Chi Building

- What is Chi Building?

Chi Building is the process of building and circulating vital energies throughout your body. Some methods of Chi Building are Chi Gong, Tai Chi, Martial Arts of various styles and even Sun-Gazing. Chi is strengthened and increased by using energies of both positive and negative polarities. Yin and Yang or the energy of the below and the energy of the above. This is my understanding of it as I have learned and taught myself through trial and error over the years. Chi Building is also accomplished by journeying with one's astral body into different realms of accumulated Chi.

Chi is a generalized term in this context for energies that increase strength, personal power and vitality. There are forms of Chi that are negative, or sickness Chi that must be expelled and replaced with the right kinds to impart maximum health and well-being.

- Why should I do Chi Building?

Chi building is an essential step or process for maintaining ones mental, spiritual, psychic and physical health. It allows a person to stay centered, feel powerful, happy, enthusiastic and able to take on any challenge in life without depression overpowering them.

Depression is often a symptom of having a low amount of Chi. Followed by other symptoms of a mental or even psychotic nature. An example is one suffering traumatic life event that caused him or her to lose a large portion of Chi by excessive unhealthy activities driven by grief or whatever intense emotion you they may have been feeling. If a person becomes very undisciplined and regresses to a state of trying to overcompensate for loss of some kind then they usually end up worse off than they were. This is why the masters say "You must master yourself first, before moving beyond a certain point." You must master your own mind or you will be destroyed by the world…not directly, but from the inside out. Your own mind will destroy you. I am not saying this to scare you. I am saying it to impress upon you the importance of Self-Mastery above all other things in the outside world. Remember, the outside is a reflection of the inside. Think about that before you build so much thought power that you literally manifest with a mere emotion driven thought.

You must do Chi Building or you will be a reed blowing in the psychic wind of the others who surround you. If you do not build your vital energies, once again…you are a "sitting duck". The world is full of powerful individuals who have the ability crush you with a passing thought because they have mastered themselves and you have not. Do not be a puff of smoke, a flash in the pan. In the words of the Daemon King Azazel …"Love not the finite pleasures, but the power you have been given over your Ego mind." Let me explain what this means exactly. Azazel is simply saying that disciplining your surface mind or ego mind is one of the most powerful steps you can take toward Self-Mastery and thus Chi Building, still it is easier said than done, given the nature of the astral realm/thought realm.

- How often should I do Chi Building?

In short, you must do it every day if possible. Do not let a day go by without some kind of centering and Chi Building. All it takes is ten minutes of Chi Gong in the morning, Sun-Gazing, or whatever works for you to keep yourself energetically healthy.

- How do I do Chi Building/How does it work? As I stated above, you can do Chi Gong, which is what I recommend at the very least. You may also do Tai Chi, Sun Gazing, or even Yoga Postures. However, *I do not recommend using Chakras to build your Chi!* Why would I say that? you may ask. Because it does not work that well for certain reasons. Some forms of yoga are fine and work great, but what you will want to avoid is working on chakras…I know this may sound crazy or new to you, but they are a way for Chi to leak out of your body, get siphoned out of your body, and even for negative Chi to get pulled into your body. I will go into this in greater detail in a later chapter. For now just trust me.

The following is a chart of the energy storage centers in the body (Chart 1). These centers are where I recommend you store your energies or Chi. They are not chakras, they are the body's natural centers of energy storage. They are not vortexes but stable energy orbs that do not leak energy unless drawn upon by you.

Chart 1
Human Energy System Without Chakras

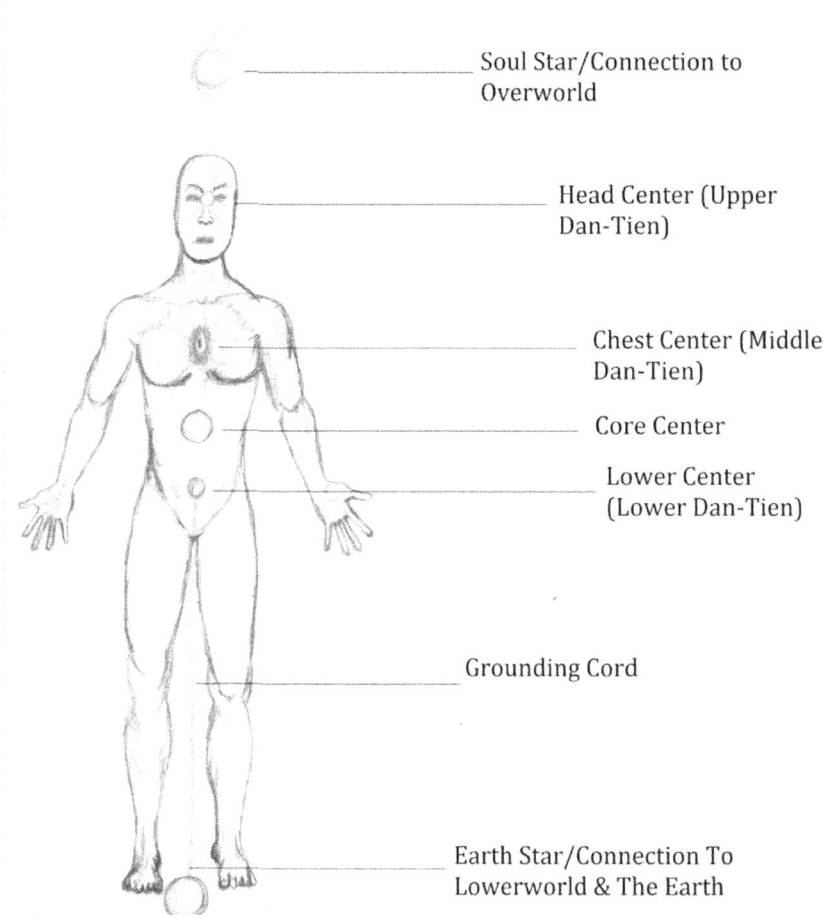

There are six energy storage centers. This is what I have found is the most accurate out of personal experience. It may be different for you. However if you are not sure of how your own energy system is naturally structured then I would use this chart as a reference guide until you become more aware of what works best for you.

First, from top to bottom is the Soul Star or connection to the Above/Overworld. This I have found is a very watery energy, or Yin Chi in the abyss like space of the Overworld. If you use the Soul Star to connect to the Sun then that is a different story. This is a Yang energy, but I will not go too deep into the different energies you will find in the Overworld just yet. The Soul Star is useful in many ways with energy work techniques as well, specifically Shielding techniques which I will go into later in this book.

The Head Center or Upper Dan-Tien is where one stores energies to help strengthen psychic abilities such as clairvoyance, telepathy, thought receiving etc. It does not matter too much what kind of Chi you store here because each of these energy storage centers are connected by the a central channel in the energy body. In Yoga this is called the Sushumna Nadi, although the name is not important. All that you need to realize is the structure and function of the energy system.

The Middle Dan-Tien or Chest Center is a great center to focus on in meditation I have found and it serves as a means of strengthening the connection of all of the energy storage centers. I call it the "Chest Center" because it is a bit above the traditional "heart" center. Also, I do not refer to it as the thymus center because it is a little deeper than where the thymus is actually located on the body not that it is necessarily tied to any physical part.

The Core Center is the center of balance and it is a good center to connect with and combine Chi of more than one kind. What I mean is that one can use both Yin and Yang together to create more powerful effects on their reality e.g. healing for themselves or another.

The Lower Center or Lower Dan-Tien is the Primary center to focus on when drawing Chi from the Earth and feeling grounded and protected.

The Earth Star is the center one sends into the Earth to synchronize their energies with Hers. To change their vibration to one of healing and balance. The Earth has a gentle Yin Chi, however one can draw Yang Chi from the Earth as well. There is obviously more to the Earth than what most people have been told I feel.

The colors of each of these centers is whatever color energy they are filled with generally speaking. I do not like to assign them specific colors for this reason. Also sometimes they may appear dark, this does not necessarily mean that there is something wrong with them or with you. Usually it means that you are storing creative, manifestation type energy or Yin energies.

In order to build the Chi in these centers you need to focus on bringing vital energies into them and compressing it into the center. I like to do this in the morning with Chi-Gong movements and breathing. You can use the various Chi Gong movements available to consciously draw energy from the sources in the world around you, such as the Sun, the Earth and the Chi in the air around you if you are in nature.

You may also draw Chi into all other areas of your body for more overall health as well. Fill your being with vital energies daily and release the old stale energies.

I do not recommend drawing Chi from the moon until you are more advanced at the process of drawing energy, especially during a full moon. The full moon is more likely to draw energy out of you than you out of it. In fact it often draws energy more so than it gives. I personally rarely use the energies of the Moon for my Magick and I will explain why in a later chapter.

If you do the Chi Gong or Tai Chi movements, you will start to feel the energy flowing pretty quick. Take your time and get a feel for it and then draw the Chi into your centers (one at a time is best.) using your hands, mind and breath to direct it.

I will explain a couple simple movements in writing for you to use. They are all you will need to get started, but please if you can, read into it further or watch some videos to learn more.

Step One:
Make sure you are grounded and stand up straight, slight bend in the knees, feet pointed slightly outward shoulder width apart.

Step Two:
Now hands out in front of you at chest level, bend at the knees and waist, and bring open palmed hands down toward the ground/floor beneath your feet as you exhale. Hands should be open and palms facing away from you. when you nearly touch the ground or floor exhale the sickness or negative Chi into the Earth to be transmuted and recycled. Then Smoothly transition into inhalation and moving upward, pulling hands in toward your body, palms begin to face toward your body as you pull them in, moving upward and inhaling pure, positive Chi.

Step Three:
As you move upward out of the squatting position move hands out in front again and upward above your head, all the while inhaling. Inhale the pure, fresh Chi through your hands into your centers. Then move back downward exhaling the negative Chi into the ground once again. Repeat this cycle to cleanse and flush your Chi energies.

The next Chi Gong exercise is one that you can transition into quickly from the last one. Same starting position. The only difference is the hand/arm positions and you will be drawing Chi in and accumulating it in your centers, one at a time.

Step One:
Begin with hands out to sides, close to your body. Hips move backwards, your back begins to arch a bit and hands move in front of you, crossing over each other with palms facing down as you lower into a squatting stance bending at the knees and at the waste.

Step Two:
Now reverse the direction coming out of the squat, hands moving laterally uncrossing and reaching up to the universe in

a "Y" shape above your head. As you inhale, breath the Chi into your hands and into the Center you wish to charge. If you are facing the Sun, draw chi from the Sun if desired. Repeat until each center gets at least one full breath of Universal Chi energy. See the energies flow into your hands, down your arms, into the torso and then the center you are charging. Repeat this cycle until you feel buzzy and energized. Repeat the Grounding exercise if you feel overly jittery.

C. Shielding

- What is Shielding?

Shielding is the practice of protecting your accumulated vital energies and Chi. It is way of defending your energy, it is not proficient by itself at completely guarding your energy, but it is a necessary step in the process of learning to protect yourself fully.

- Why should I do Shielding?

The more Chi or Vital Energy that you have, the greater the likely hood that someone or something in the astral plane or physical plane will try to steal it or take it from you through manipulation or psychic vampirism. For this reason, it is necessary to protect your energies from this and other forms of energetic attack.

Not only will Shielding provide some protection from vampiric/draining attacks, it will guard you from your enemies who may be launching Magickal attacks at you as well. It does not matter what their path is. If a person hates you, is envious of you, fears you in some way or is trying to keep you down, they will often launch a Magickal attack especially if they know you have no defenses. If you have no magickal defense, it means that there is no risk of the their attacks being deflected back to them. If you have Shielding however, it is likely to deflect at least some of their attack back to them. They will then think twice before attacking you with Magick again. Astral entities can use Magick on you as well and their attacks are often quite stealthy and hard to notice until it is too late to block them. With shielding the damage done to your subtle body can be mitigated to a degree.

The most important reason for Shielding is not protection from other people or other Magickians, Witches, or Sorcerers though. It is for protection from the Parasites that use the Matrix we live in to feed on us throughout our lives without our ever even realizing it. Now I am sure this sounds like a very audacious and wild statement to you if you are not fully aware of what transpires in the astral plane. I am not trying to scare you. I will go into detail about these beings in a later chapter, but for now just trust me, take it one step at a time and shield your energies from them.

- How do I do Shielding/How does it work?

The way I do shielding is by using some of the Chi I have accumulated by shaping it and programming it with my intention and words. We however must use the Chi in a way that is a bit more advanced for best results. I will guide you step by step in this process. Read carefully and practice each step until you get it right. Once you do it a few times, it will seem much quicker and easier than the initial couple times. It becomes much easier once you commit the steps to memory. If you want, you may write the steps down in a abridged version for easier practice and memorization.

Step One:
Do grounding and Chi Building to start, as described earlier and remain in a standing position for best results.

Step Two:
Now I want you to stand facing the Sun in the sky. Even if you are indoors, the Sun still permeates any barriers between you and it, when you focus on it. Talk to the Sun as if he were conscious (He is indeed conscious.) the same as you did the Earth. The Sun is a powerful Yang Chi and it will serve to strengthen your aura effectively. If you must name the Sun, I recommend calling him Sekhmet (Who is actually a female manifestation.), Ra, Sorath, Lugh, or even Horus. These are different Spirits that have been born of the Sun as a way he or

she could interact with us in form. Research them and choose one you are most drawn to. Note, the Sun can be male or female in essence.

If it is Dawn or Dusk stand with eyes open gazing directly at the Sun as you connect. Do not overdo this part if you have not Sungazed before. Take it slow.

Step Three:
Once you feel a good connection to the Sun, speak your intention. "It is my wish to accumulate your Chi into my energy system for protection." Or something to this effect. Remember Gratitude, after you start receiving a charge. Feel the energy beam down through the crown of your head from the Soul Star which connects to the Sun. If you are proficient with clairvoyance or even visualization then the energy looks just like concentrated Sun light as it beams to you. It is intense white light.

Step Four:
Accumulate the Solar Chi into your Chi Centers one at a time. Once you reach the position where the Earth Star would normally be (It is now in the womb of the Earth because you grounded... right?), create a node or axis point for the energy to collect in this same spot. This should be just below the feet on the grounding cord. Use a Circular shape when creating the node. Once you accumulate a good amount of Solar Chi into the node proceed to Step Five.

Step Five:
The energy continues to flow into the node because of your concentration and focus on this occurrence until it is so full that it bursts outward into an oval bubble of Yang Chi Light around your body and immediate aura, all the way up to the Soul Star, where it connects. A circuit of energy is created that is so strong and seamless it is impossible for anything negative to penetrate it without passing through the bubble of Yang Chi Light, which is not possible. Hold this visualization and feeling of being encompassed in this protective energy. Feel the waves continue to flow from the node up to the Soul Star

in the oval shape. You may use your arms to direct the energy the same way you would doing Chi Gong exercises. It is after all, Chi Energy you are using.

Step Six:
With your intention still fully focused on this oval shaped shield, state the following out loud to the energy itself to program it. ***"It is my Will to be protected from harmful and intrusive energies, psychic and physical attacks, energy loss and leakage, frequency control, astral hooks, psychic vampirism, curses, hexes, bindings, mental or emotional manipulation, blank-slate technologies, mind control, Implants, Archons and Astral Parasites!!!"***

Or if you wish you may simply say. ***"It is my Will to be protected from all negativity and all harm"***

Say these words with absolute conviction and intention…push your emotions into this statement for powerful results.

You may stop here or if you need greater/more advanced protection then continue with the following next steps. Remember to thank the Sun at this point for the abundant Chi.

Step Seven:
Sense your Earth Star deep in the womb of the Earth. The Earth Star should be surrounded by a magnetic green energy, it is a watery energy. Sense this energy all around your Earth Star. Sense the roots of your Earth star extending and gathering this liquid energy into itself. It will flow into your legs and then into your Energy Storage Centers one at a time. Because these already have a charge of Yang Chi allow this Yin energy to surround the Yang energy. It encircles it like a large orb covering a smaller orb. Proceed to each Energy Storage Center and surround one at a time with the energy.

Step Eight:
Bring this Yin Earth Chi up to the Soul Star. Build up a strong charge here. Then when you are ready let the energy burst down around the Yang Chi Oval Shield that is already in place. Let the Yin energy surround it completely all the way down to the node at the bottom. Hold this visualization and feeling. Feel and see the energy flow down from the Soul Star in waves until a thick powerful electromagnetic shield is now formed.

Step Nine:
Commence the programming or intention statement once again. ***"It is my Will to be protected from harmful and intrusive energies, psychic and physical attacks, energy loss and leakage, frequency control, astral hooks, psychic vampirism, curses, hexes, bindings, mental or emotional manipulation, blank-slate technologies, mind control, Implants, Archons and Astral Parasites!!!"***
Or you may say: ***"It is my Will to be protected from all negativity and harm"***

This time add extra measures if you desire. For example you may want to "Deflect curses or hexes back to the sender." If you are getting hit with Magickal attack. however It is more likely the case that strong astral parasites may try to drain you and manipulate you though. You may add extra protection against these forces if desired as well. These are just examples of what you may do and may not be necessary on a daily basis. Use your intuition and be guided to what your needs may be each day. Also you may put up both shield layers then program them both at the same time rather than programming twice. Do this in order to save time.

In addition to these extra measures, I have received what are called Words of Power to amplify the Shielding if desired. You may chant or sing the word "BHS-LABC" (Pronounced Buh-Hah-Suh-Luh-ah-Buh-Cuh), you may also say the word silently in your head if you wish. This Word of Power was received from Sekhmet and will add her protective Goddess energy to your shielding. Chant her name then the Word for a more powerful effect.

You may chant the Word of Power after the shield is in place to amp it up, or anytime during the day to recharge it. Do not forget to thank Sekhmet if you use the Word of Power. A little Gratitude goes a long way. For more Words of Power and further instruction on their use refer to my Book ***Grimoire Of The Neteru.***

Chart 2 below is an example of what a fully charged double layered shield looks like if you were visualizing it or viewing it clairvoyantly. It shows a double layered Protection Shield that is utilizing golden or red Yang Chi and A surrounding layer of green or blue Yin Chi for effective protection from negative energies. The colors are not necessarily exactly what you will see. The actual color of the Solar chi is much brighter than I can show with black and white images, but the purpose here is to show you where each layer must be placed. The feminine Yin Surrounds the Masculine Yang. I would like to add that you may experiment with different kinds of energy on your own to create the best combination of effects for you.

Chart 2
Double Layered Protection Shield

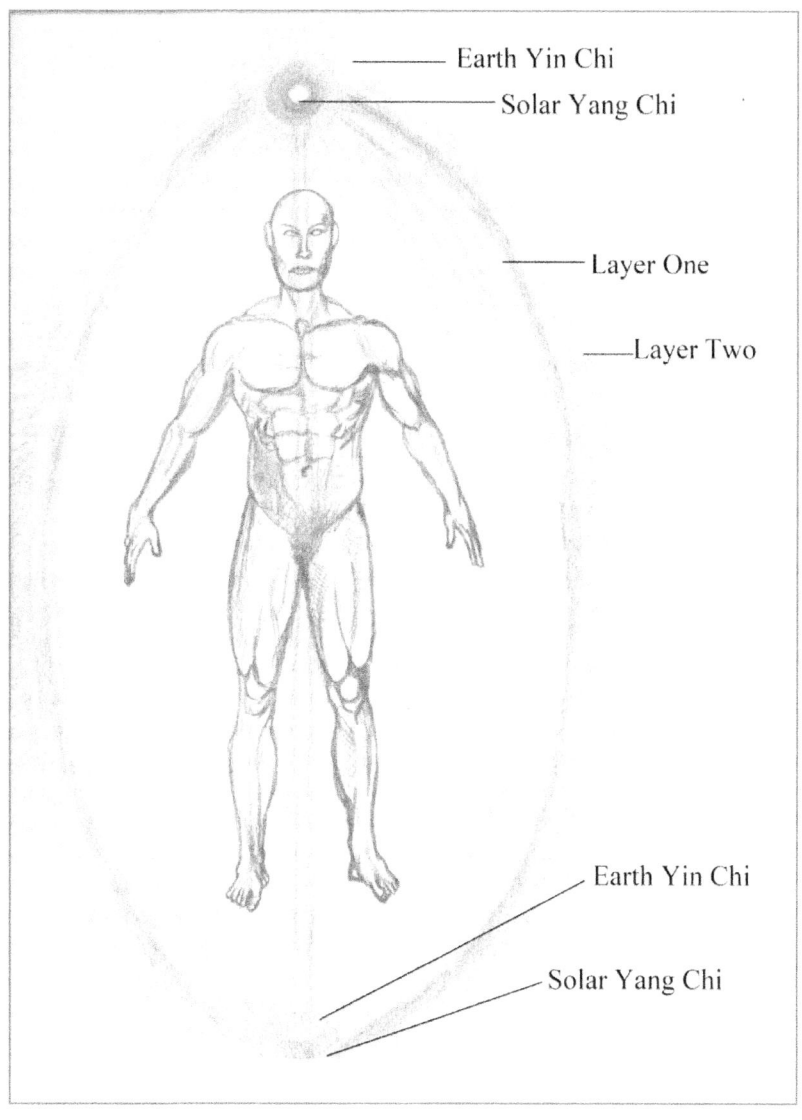

D. Meditation

- What is Meditation?

Meditation is primarily the practice or technique of slowing the thoughts of the surface mind and entering an altered state in order to access the subconscious and various different layers of the mind, and even the spirit plane if desired. This is my own take on what meditation is. I am not regurgitating words from another book. My goal here is to keep this simple and understandable. Thus I choose to tell you what it is from my personal experience rather than using someone else's words or ideas. Secondly, it is allowing all Negative Ego thoughts to cease in order to have a state of awareness of what we are at deeper levels. To have awareness of your true Self.

- Why should I Meditate?

I believe meditation is an essential tool for a successful life. What success is to each individual is obviously different. What I mean when I say "success" is that an individual lives the life that they desire, that they accomplish their most cherished dreams. If you can do this, then you are a successful person. Meditation has tremendous benefits for mental and emotional health and well-being. Meditation is a cornerstone for all spiritual or Magickal practice to be successful. Do not miss out on this powerful tool in your own health and Energy Management. Do not fail to manifest your dreams for this life because you were afraid that you were not able to meditate.

- How do I Meditate/How does it Work?

I get asked very often "how do I meditate?" or many people say to me, "I can't meditate…" and they believe it to such a degree that it becomes true for them, sadly. What I am trying to say is that if you read this section step by step and do not get discouraged or overwhelmed by it, you will have success at meditating. It is very easy to meditate if you are not afraid to do it *imperfectly*. If you expect to be perfect at it from the first try then you are just asking to feel like a failure and give up. Meditation requires consistency, tenacity and an attitude of positivity at all times.

The mind is tricky, it knows when you are fighting it and overthrowing it's hold on you and your life. The first day you begin to meditate you will be repelled by it. Your mind will come up with many reasons why you "can't meditate" and you will be tempted to believe them. What I want you to do is realize that they are all excuses. It is all bullshit. Understand? Seriously your mind is full of shit. Specifically your negative ego as I call it.

The negative ego is the part of your surface mind that tells you lies about what you can and cannot do. It will tell you that you are not good enough to do this or that. It will tell you that others are going to think you are stupid, dumb, annoying, awkward etc. Listen to me when I tell you again…*It's all bullshit*. It lives on a doubt and fear emotional frequency and thus it will do everything it can to keep itself fed on your insecurities. It is not easily ignored or controlled. Not because you are not strong , but because of outside influences/factors effecting your mind. More on this in later chapters.

I am going to outline a simple meditation method for this step in Energy Management. There are many ways of meditating, but I am not going to confuse you and tell you all the different ways. If you are new to meditating, you will just feel overwhelmed. I ask you to stick with what I show you here for at least three months of consistent, daily practice. Do not deviate at all. Do not take a day off. Even if you only have time for five minutes, you must do it. And that is how I want you to think. Think, "I must do it" do not think "I should do it." The moment you "should" your meditation, it automatically becomes a non-priority and you fail to do it.

Do not get me wrong, there is wiggle room for days when things happen that stop you from doing meditation at the same specific time. If this happens do it later in the day as long as you do it. Also, once you are able to meditate consistently you are allowed breaks to do/learn other things that come up. What I mean is that if you are doing Ritual Magick for example and meditation of some kind is a step in the Ritual (which it usually is) then that counts as your meditation. Another thing that counts is journeying or astral travel because it requires preliminary meditation steps to be successful at. However if you can, meditate everyday as part of your daily Energy Management practices.

Keep in mind that the daily Energy Management practices are written in this book in order of priority and importance. "A" is the first thing you should do if you have no time to do everything else. If you have time to do two Energy Management Practices outlined choose "A" Grounding and "B" Chi Building before doing "C" Shielding etc. Just make sure your intention is to replace the old shield when you do Shielding. Your shield should remain from the day before until you get the chance to replace it with fresh energy.

Now for the meditation that I want you to start with. This is a simple but very effective meditation that will keep you balanced every day. I will provide different meditations in other books, but for now use this meditation as a foundational method. It will have psychic effects such as, spontaneous astral travel from dream state, thought receiving, increases in intuition, telepathy with spirit (talking to Spirit during the meditation) to name a few.

Issues will arise with all of these psychic powers because of the influence of the negative ego and the outside influences I mentioned earlier. This will try to confuse you and make you feel delusional. Indeed you may become delusional at times, until I show you how to break free of the Energy Extraction Cycle I call it. I will go into this in detail in later steps in this book. You will need to read these steps and learn everything in this book if you hope to be effective in using psychic ability. If you do not learn the tools here, you will be confused and get messed with until you do. One step at a time learn and grow with the tools in this book and you will get there.

Step One:
After you are grounded, have built Chi and are shielded, sit down, back straight on a comfortable chair. No recliners, they will cause your back to slouch. The key is to be comfortable and still stay awake. We want a trance, not sleep. You need to remember what transpires during the meditation if you can.

Feet flat on the floor. No lotus posture, just simple comfortable sitting. Hands resting on knees with palms facing up. Thumbs touching index finger, middle finger or both together. Close your eyes.

Step Two:
Begin to breathe through your nose if you can, mouth only if you have allergies or you just cannot breath through your nose for some reason. Take Nettle Root if you have allergies, it may help. Slow, calm inhale expanding lower abdomen first, chest then upper chest. Be sure you are breathing with your belly for maximum relaxation effects. Exhale through nose twice the length of time as your inhale. I am not going to give a specific length of time, I only suggest that you inhale slowly and exhale twice as slowly ok.

Step Three:
Place your awareness on your Middle Dan-Tien. It is located behind the lower portion of your thymus gland as shown on Chart 1. You may visualize it as a white light surrounded by a blue hue. It may be visualized as a flame or even an oval orb. It may be visualized as a purple-blue flame or light also, purple center and blue outer layer, or at times black center and light on the outside. Connect with it, breathe slowly holding it in your awareness.

Step Four:
Meditate on this center. Let go of all other thoughts and pay attention only to breath and this center. It burns with power, it glows and grows in intensity the longer you hold it in your mind. Remember, other thoughts will come, let them come and let them go. If you lose focus, all you need to do is refocus

your attention gently without anger or judgment on yourself. One step at a time. One day at a time you will improve.

Step Five: After holding the center in your mind for at least ten minutes, twenty minutes if time permits; allow it to grow slowly as you exhale, holding its oval/flame shape. See it grow and immolate your entire body and immediate aura. It should extend at least two feet from your body on all sides in its oval flame shape. Hold it here for another five to ten minutes. You may choose to expand it further out to about five feet on all sides, but keep in mind it will cause you to connect with people around you energetically even when you are not intending to. If this happens and it is not desired, then pull it back in a few feet.

Step Six:
Thank the Universe and close the meditation. We thank the Universe because we are the Universe. Meditating on this center strengthens your connection to your Inter-Dimensional-Self. The part of you that is one-hundred percent Universe. It is the real you. Everything we do in this book is toward aligning with Her and being one with Her in a way.

This completes the basic steps of Energy Management. The following chapters will outline the importance of Magickal Practice from a Left-Hand-Path perspective. They are essential to maintenance and growth. Magickal Practice is a very important key to your health, growth, protection and defense as an awakened being. If you do not move into the next steps, your progress will eventually hit a plateau.

If you take the time to read this book of Soul-Retrieval in its entirety and to understand what Soul-Retrieval really is, and what you are up against in this world, You will break new ground quickly and experience greater spiritual growth. Certain elements of this world or reality are here to keep you locked in fear and pain. These enemies will not stop harming you because you are a positive, loving person. For this reason more directly oppositional actions are needed.

Chapter 2
Gratitude For Life

I have placed gratitude in its own chapter primarily to emphasize its importance in everyday life. Really it is a basic of Energy Management, but I feel it should receive full focus for a few good pages. Gratitude is important because of the way the Universe is, not necessarily because of moral constructs of right and wrong.

The Universe or the world we live in is a machine in how it works. It creates for you what you put out to it. This is a basic law of metaphysics, It is a Hermetic Principle and can be found in the Bible, in the Emerald Tablets of Thoth and in many new age books out there today. It works in practice and it is a foundation of creating your ideal life. It must be practiced every day or you will miss out on so much opportunity in your life.

It is not religious or dogmatic in any way. It is not even necessarily spiritual. It is a technique or tool to make your life better. It is not worshiping anything or anybody. It is not groveling, nor is it giving your power away. Realize that the Universe that you are grateful to is one hundred percent you. It is a part of you. You are thanking the source of your being. Why not thank yourself for everything good in your life that you can think of. Thank yourself for all the good things that you do not even have yet. Thank the Universe for the love that you will receive, for gifts that you will receive. Thank her for giving you freedom from the enslavement of the Energy Extraction Matrix.

The more gratitude that you have the more the Universe will continue to give to you and bless you. Thank her for increases in material wealth and for increases in spiritual wealth. It is important to do this every day. Be thankful everyday for what you have and what you will have.

I personally keep what I call a Gratitude Journal. In this Journal I write down everything I can think of that I am grateful for. This automatically puts me in a good mood for the day. I state out loud what I am grateful for to the Universe at least once a day, reading from my Gratitude Journal. It is an easy way to remember what you are grateful for, even if you are in a bad mood, which is when gratitude is needed the most. Bad days come to test you and see if you will give in to the negativity. If you prevail and stay positive things always get better, trust me.

Gratitude is also important If you work with spirits, spirit guides, daemons, faye, elemental spirits, ancestral spirits, the dead, the shades of the dead, or any kind of spirit that helps you, then I recommend that you be grateful to them in a vocal way. Do not push them around and expect them to serve you and be your slaves. This is a mistake and will blow up in your face.

Always be grateful for the gifts that you receive. Be grateful for things you have earned as well. That is the opportunity to earn these good things. Do not take what you have for granted. Do not ever complain. Words are powerful spells. Even if you are joking and you think it is funny to do self-deprecating humor, do not do it. It is complaining and stating in words that you are this or that. The words you use change your reality.

Words are symbols with specific meanings…despite your intention, the meaning is there and has an effect. This is Spell-work in a basic form. It affects reality. It is not a thing to take lightly.

Although there are many funny T.V. shows and movies that program us to act funny with depreciating humor or self-loathing humor we should not follow the T.V. and act like we do not love ourselves just to be funny. Do not put people down to be funny. It still effects them…even if they laugh they are belittled inside.

The T.V. is not reality, it is programming. It is a tool used by government and false leaders to make us dumb and numb. Your life is not what you are told it is by the T.V. or whatever other media you watch or listen to.

What I am saying in a roundabout way is know your exact intention and use words that match that intention to the best of your ability. This includes statements of gratitude.

Do not be overly general in expressing gratitude. Does a lover like to hear you say "thanks for everything" over and over again every day, when they do amazingly thoughtful and specific things for you? NO, they want to know that you noticed that extra attention they put into loving you in little detailed ways. You are a microcosm, correct? You are a manifestation of the whole Universe in a smaller form, correct? Thus the Universe will respond to your noticing the little things that others take for granted. It is what makes you special to Her. Thank Her for all the little things that happen throughout your day and see how your life changes.

Do not forget to thank her for this book and for the important information you are learning that will alter your life for the better. I say this to give you the greatest chance of successfully understanding this book and gaining all the power of your Inter-Dimensional-Self in your life. Be grateful for every step you successfully take on the ladder of ascension toward Embodiment.

You should know that Gratitude is more than words. It is an attitude of optimism. It is an exuberant emotion of feeling overwhelmed with good vibes. When you achieve a goal that you have been working on for a good amount of time with consistency and with help from spirit and or the Universe. Give it to Them, give it to Her. Do not feel grateful and hold it in. Express it with heartfelt meaning. Let it overflow into the world around you. Let it be known how much you love to be happy and free of negativity.

These moments will come in your life. These moments will come as you work through this book. When they do, do not be stingy, speak up! Love the Universe for loving you.

Chapter 3
Enemies

Remember when I said that there are outside influences that you will have to tackle if you want to grow beyond basics? This is where I tell you what those are. First we will start with the less threatening ones and then I will describe the more powerful and hard to get rid of influences that you will need to contend with.

Common Intrusive Energy

For starters there are many smaller energy draining Astral Parasites out there that you must protect yourself from. These usually appear in the mind's eye as a rodent (Rat, or other creeper) or various types of insects. At times they appear as a formless blob of energy…these are often man-made thought forms gone awry. All astral parasitic energies feed on low frequency emotions and feelings. Because of this they do everything that they can to exacerbate a negative emotion or feeling that person may have. They look for weaknesses, fears, doubts, pain in the body, depression, you name it. Any emotion/feeling that is low frequency and is causing you to suffer.

As a Reiki Master and Chi Energy Healer I find these astral parasites lodged in my the energy bodies of my clientele often and even in my own energy body at times. They are easily removed once you place attention on them and realize their presence. Usually the energy body has been damaged and needs healing/repairing after a removal of such an entity though.

If you are suffering from unexplainable, non-stop anxiety or depression I personally do not recommend taking pills and getting therapy before you check your energy body for these entities and learn the steps of Energy-Management. If your symptoms are energetic you will feel better almost immediately after you do the Energy Management Work. If you do not feel better there is more to be learned still before resorting to being on medication the rest of your life. Please continue step by step through this book.

Archons

The next on the list of Astral Parasites is what are most commonly known as Archon type parasites. These are known as Archons because they fit the description of certain beings in Gnostic scriptures and texts. I am not trying to creep you out, but you must be aware of your enemies or you will have trouble in your spiritual growth process. The enemies are there, no matter how much you focus on "love and light" they will continue to prey on you while you are sleeping. I mean this literally and metaphorically just to clarify. There are a few types I have come across in my own growth. I will explain one by one.

One:
Drone Arachnid type-These suckers are what you will most commonly find draining you while you are sleeping. They look like big, flat-black or gray spiders. I remember the first time I found one on me as a child. I awoke and sat up in bed. My astral vision was still on. It came from the corner of my bed and crawled up my arm… it was a huge spider shape. I was terrified and screamed for my mother. When she arrived the Drone vanished, because I was fully awake by the time my mother was holding me. "Just a bad dream…" she said, I wished that were true. These entities seem to be more prevalent than ever today, crawling all over their sleeping prey. Perhaps they are part of the reason that people have such a hard time sleeping at night, and why they feel so tired the next day. Drone type archons such as these will often enter your dream plane and directly penetrate your astral body. The

most common area they penetrate from my experience is the heart center. Creating jealousy, hatred, envy and every other heart related emotional issue possible in the dayside reality. For example you may feel insecure in your relationship no matter what, because they are stuck inside your body creating these feelings and feeding on you.

If you have had a dream of a large black spider pouncing on you and burrowing into you, then you may be a victim of this Arachnid Type archon.

Two:
Floating Type, With Tendrils-These are also very common and look like a big, flat-black or gray floating squid with tendrils used to pierce your aura and suck your energy. They do not burrow into you. They float beside or above and hook your aura or energy body with a tendril. These are quite prevalent in daily life. This is why I included "astral hooks" in the Shielding statement in the Energy Management section of the book. They may come in an organic form or machine like inorganic form.

Three:
Humanoid Type with Tendrils-These particular Archon Type Parasites have arms and legs and look human shaped. They have tendrils all over their bodies that slither all around them looking to feed. They also have the ability to speak in English. Most commonly threatening words when you realize that they are present. Their voices are raspy, gurgley and frightening. They are not as common, but will show up once you kick out their inferiors or drones. They look organic so far I have seen.

I will show you how to deal with these beings. Unfortunately they are not as easy to get rid of as the other astral parasites that are around. They require the use of powerful Magick to break free of them with finality.

Four:
Spinal Implant Type-This is where the shit gets real disturbing. These entities legit hack your brain and vital energy system by implanting themselves in your spinal cord and Central Nervous System primarily to filter out their detection from your awareness. I mean this in the astral sense only, for those who may take this out of context. They keep you asleep like a good sheep. Disgusting to think about really. I have specific ways to rid them from your body and mind completely. They can literally wipe your thoughts of their existence. They take your attention off themselves and make you do things that are all about ego mind…eat, fuck, sleep. These are the ones responsible for mind control activity. Sounds crazy I know, but it will not hurt to try to clear yourself of them whether you believe they are real or not. Personally I did a cursing Rite to rid them of my mind. That same night after falling asleep I saw them in my dream getting pulled out of my brainstem (of my subtle body)…it was supremely disturbing, but I am super happy to have my mind wide awake and in my own control. I will go into detail later on how you can do the same if you wish.

One final important thing you should know about Archon Type Parasites is that they are expert mimics. If you have your mind's eye open as many people do these days, they will mimic the image or voice of another Magickian or Witch and try to trick you into believing that they are psychically or Magickally attacking you. Often they succeed and get allies or friends to curse each other. I hope my fellow Magickians and Witches out there who read this will see that we are not each other's enemies. I urge other Witches and Magickians to make sure they are free of Archonic/Parasitic influences. If you wish to use a curse on something then it's open season on all archons. These Astral Suckers have been eating human energy for a long time and it is time we fought back! I urge you to curse these parasites who are feeding on your family and friends.

Archons will also try to mimic the telepathy ability of loved ones as well, to stir up trouble and negativity in order to destroy harmony. They do this so they can feed.

I do want to make sure the reader understands that these spirits are not Deamons. Daemons are not what you have been taught if you are new to Magickal Practice. They are like you and me. They are like people. Some are good, some are not helpful. I have honestly learned more from Daemons than I ever could from any Angelic force. If it were not for the wisdom of the Daemonic I would still be a mindless victim of circumstance. I have them to thank for my freedoms, my health and my well-being. Specifically the Egyptian Gods/Goddesses/Neteru, The Arch-Daemons of the Qlipoth and The Daemon King Azazel. Their help has led to the writing of this book and if you trust me and them, you will be helped as well.

The following sketches are of the Different Archon types that I, and my sibling Sara, have encountered.

Sketch One
Drones

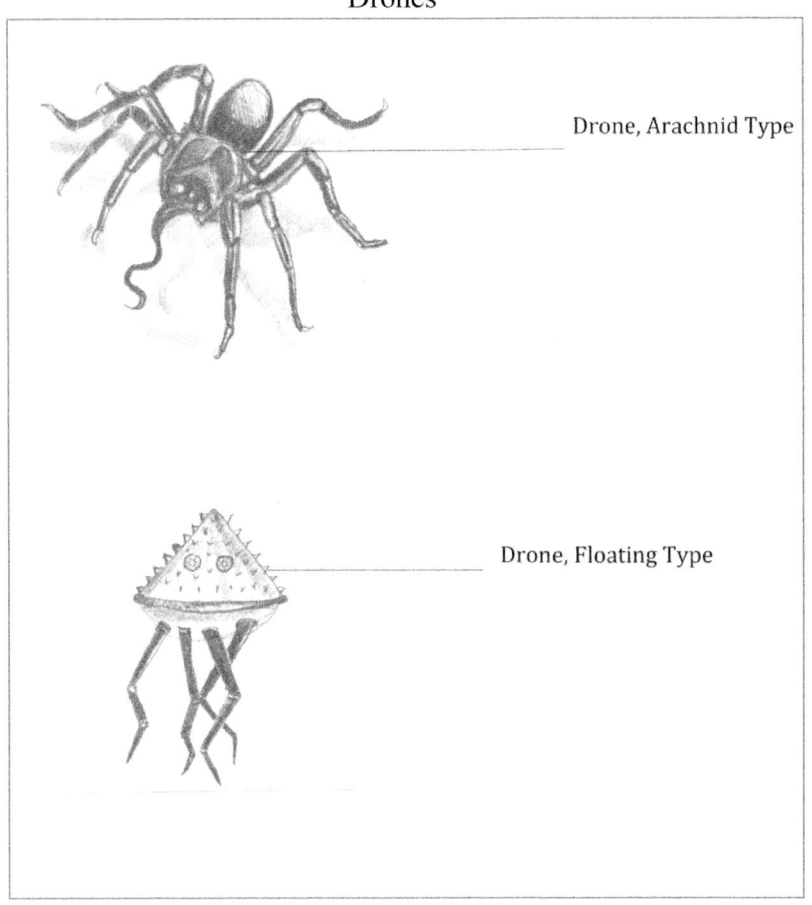

Sketch Two
Spinal Implant Drone

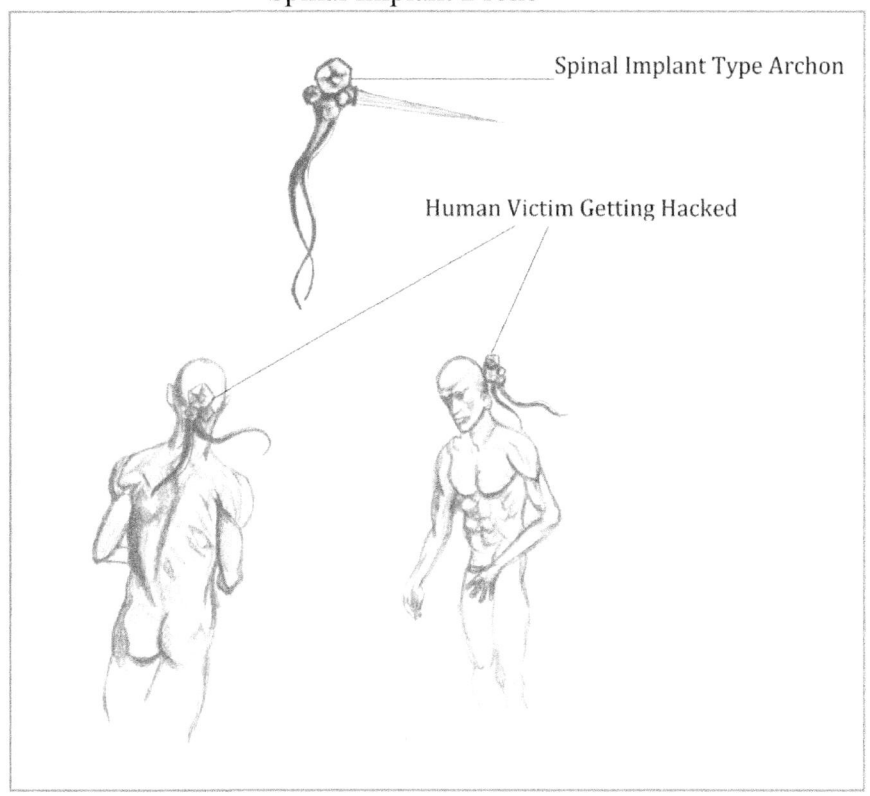

Sketch Three
Floating Type With Tendrils

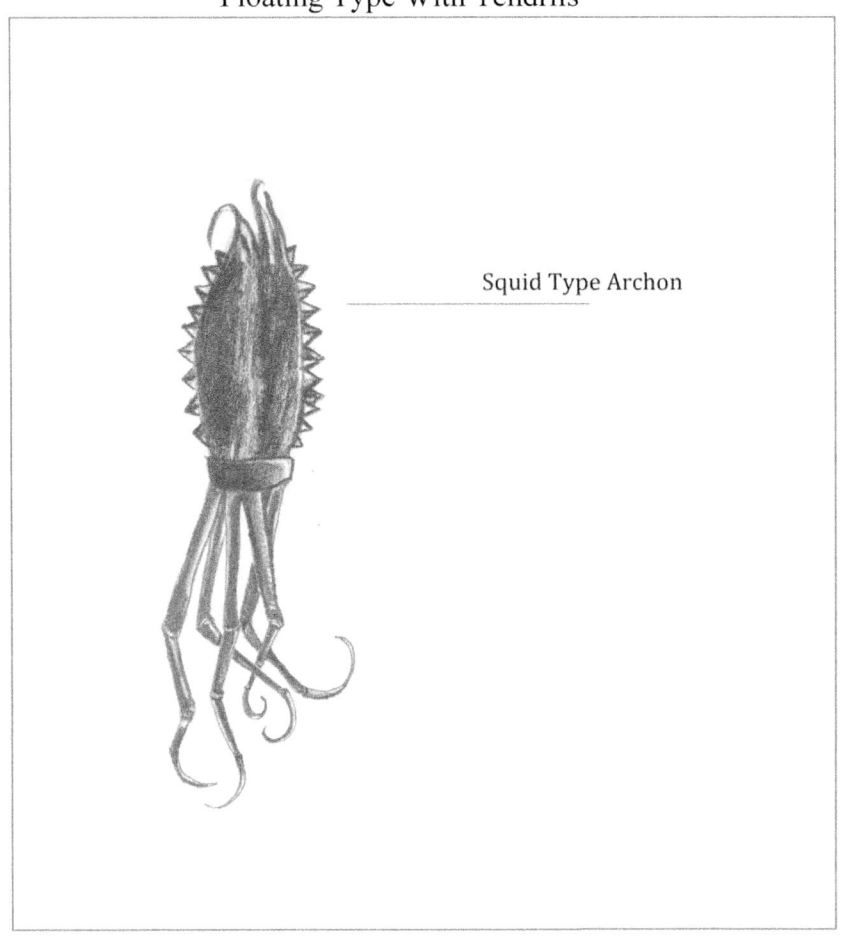

Squid Type Archon

Sketch Four
Humanoid Type With Tendrils

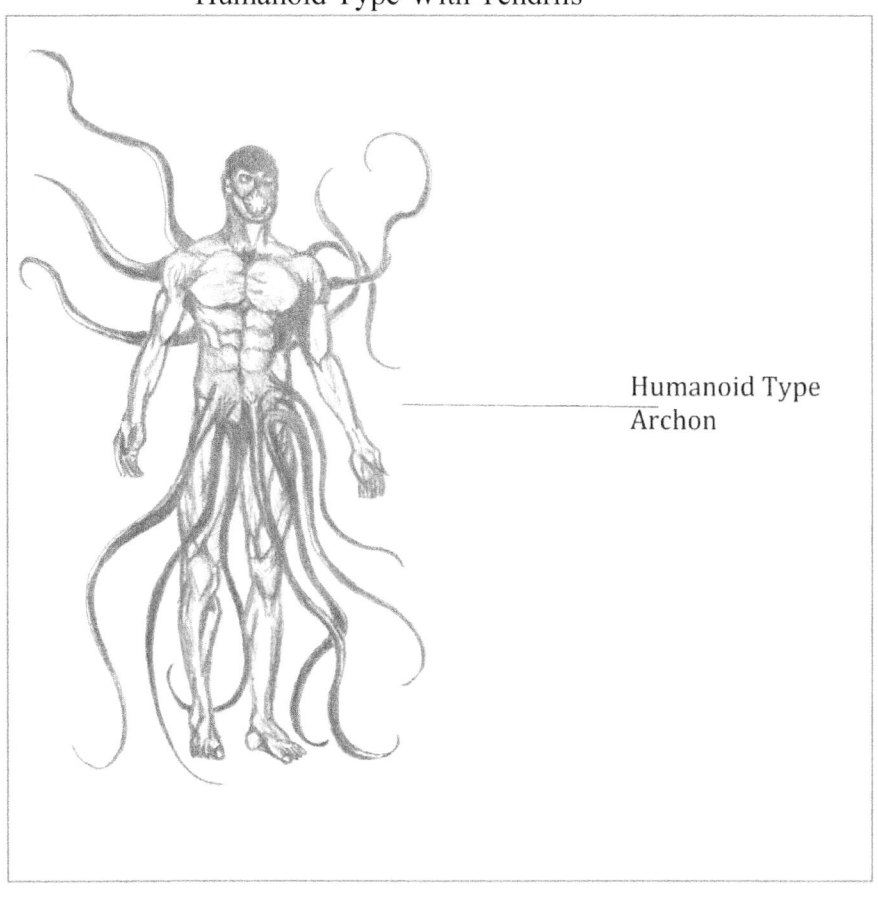

Humanoid Type Archon

The Controllers

Another enemy that you must be aware of are what I call the Controllers. These are inter-dimensional beings that are able to work outside of time or use time travel to keep humans enslaved. They live in a dimension of non-time. From this vantage point they often insert control programs into the timeline in order to keep the average person in a state of control and drone mentality. They have done this successfully for a long "time" if you will, but that "time" if I may, is coming to an end.

I am giving you knowledge that I wish I had many years ago. I would make a little progress and get knocked down again and again because I could not see these beings behind the veil setting traps for me…I knew within myself that I could not give up. I stayed consistent in my battle against these beings without knowing that they existed…no easy task. My point is that you now have the information that I suffered and struggled to gain for many years. Use it wisely.

These beings are the ones usually responsible for so called alien abduction cases. But really they are not aliens in the sense of the word being used. They are alien to this plane yes, but not from other planets necessarily. There appearance is like that of a typical Gray alien except taller. They have very large heads and big black eyes. Usually they have a high collar that extends half way up the length of their large heads, but not always.

Later in this book, during Soul-Retrieval Rites, you may find that these beings are responsible for fragmenting your soul. They abduct parts of our souls while we are asleep. This is why so many people experience alien abduction dreams that are very lucid…like they are actually occurring. It is because they are actually occurring to your soul or subtle body. A fragment of it is taken and used to create emotions of despair and terror which they feed on. This is why Soul-Retrieval is needed for humanity now more than ever.

Typical Appearance of a Controller

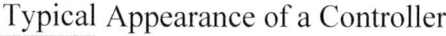

Keep in mind however that there are other tribes of this type of being that are friendly. For example my spirit guide "Mike" looks quite similar, but is not the same as these Controllers. He is of a different "tribe" and is not here to harm humans.

You should be able to tell if they are harmful or not based on how you feel in their presence. Listen to your gut. They will do everything that they can to confuse you and throw you off course. They want your fears and self doubts to take over and ruin your spiritual progress. Some people are able to easily tune these beings out and ignore them. This is a good way of protecting your mind from their influence. I personally have to take a more active approach for whatever reason; my sensitivity or awareness of them perhaps.

The Reptilians

The Reptilians are as much astral entities as they are physical ones. They seem to be in alliance with the Controllers and some secret government organizations. They have a humanoid shape like the Controllers but normal sized heads (although some have larger heads). Their skin is covered in yellow, green and black scales like a serpent or lizard. They are also inter-dimensional entities who are outside of the Earth time spaces. You will likely have to battle them along with the Controllers with the Rites that are provided in later chapters in order to claim more spiritual freedoms and growth. These beings are usually hostile toward humans, but this is not an absolute. There are a few Reptilian groups that may not be enemies of humans, but for the most part, one can safely assume that they are an enemy if you run into one of them during this work. They look at humans as cattle. Like we are their food. They will often interfere when you are trying to gain a higher vibration through meditation or ritual such as the ones found in this and other books that are about spiritual empowerment. If you encounter one, be very leery. Do not be fooled by it's lies and deceptions. Get it out of your space immediately.

Typical Appearance of a Reptilian

Chapter 4
Embodiment

The word "embodiment" is misleading to describe what this chapter is actually about. Let me explain. Embodiment sounds like something you do once and then you are good to go. In actuality it is a choice we make every single day that we wake up. We choose to walk in alignment with our Spirit, Daemon, Holy Guardian Angel, The Bornless One, or to use a term that I have coined for my own purposes and books, The Inter-Dimensional-Self.

The Inter-Dimensional-Self is a label that I choose to use because I feel it best fits the nature of my infinite Self, who is beyond time and limitation. He/She knows what is happening beyond the limitations of any dimensional space, or border of gross matter and time. The second reason I use this particular label is because this being is not my "Higher-Self" but rather he or she is me. They are not better than me or more powerful than me, they simply have a bird's eye view of my life in the confines of time and space. They see the infinite lifetimes I have lived and will continue to live here and on the other side of the plane of Earth. These lifetimes are not occurring in a linear way, but are happening concomitantly. Remember, time is not linear…this is important to understand. It is not theory, it's a fact my friends.

> Why/How must I live in alignment with my Inter-Dimensional-Self?

The reason is quite simple, however, doing it is a different story. Let us start with the " reason". We must live in alignment with our I.D.S. if we ever hope to overthrow limitation such as fear and doubt in our lives. These psychological limitations are what causes us to flop and lose sight of our inner desires and dreams for our lives. The inner desires and dreams within our hearts are what keeps us awake, alive, happy, and able to keep progressing in life. Without this inner absolute conviction that we have a purpose here and love for doing this purpose then we begin to stagnate, then fade from ourselves. What I mean is we *Fall Asleep*. We become zombies that eat, shit, sleep, work our slave jobs, watch our "programming" on the media devices and then we die. That does not sound like much of a satisfying existence to me…how about you?

What living in alignment does for us is break the negative ego hold on us. You will live in a way that is true to yourself and be truly happy and fulfilled. You will easily find strength to consistently work toward your life tasks or hearts desires without flinching because of petty life drama and distractions that do not matter. When you find this strength it will never leave you, it is there at all times and no matter how much life tries to make you lose faith, it remains a stable anchor within. You always know that you are powerful.

If you consistently live in alignment with the I.D.S. you will eventually break barriers that you previously thought impossible to ever conquer in your life. If you have an addiction for example that is causing you to feel out of whack daily then you will find strength to conquer it using the Power of your I.D.S. Again it is an anchor within you, a stable, centered anchor that is there always.

Once you reach a certain point of connectedness with your I.D.S. you will be tested and given opportunities to break free of the alignment and live in a way that gratifies only the negative ego as well as feeding the Archonic and astral parasites that dwell in this realm. I suggest that you remain true to Him/Her or you will just feel like a failure. You will know that you are out of alignment and it will haunt you until you stand back up and try again and again, until you get it right every day.

With that said, once you get to a certain point of growth through living in alignment you must be ready to sacrifice your limited ego self. Understand that this is a step by step, difficult thing to do. In Witchcraft we think back to the story of Cain and Abel. Cain slew Abel…this is viewed as completely allegorical or symbolic in my mind. Abel, being simple, ignorant, and doing whatever those around him commanded him to do was in actuality the same individual as Cain before he awoke his Inter-Dimensional-Self.

Once Cain was awakened…there was no turning back. There was no way to return to ignorant innocence and keep living a lie. He had to end the Old Self with finality. He killed him as on offering to his Daemon. His Daemon being exactly the same thing as the I.D.S., but I am getting ahead of myself here. My point is that mainstream views are backwards…many so called bad things are good things in actuality but they are hidden. They are there for you to find in the hidden dark places where it is taboo for you to explore.

Living in alignment is also important for your Magickal development and protection. The greater your level of alignment, the greater your authority over the world around you. The reason is that you are becoming the only God that is. Understand what I mean by this, I mean that you are the only authority that you must listen to ultimately. At least inwardly, always listen exclusively to your I.D.S. or you will feel like you are suffocating your hearts voice.

Now keep in mind the I.D.S. uses the external world to speak to you at times. Keep listening to Her/Him and little by little your connection and level of merging/embodiment becomes greater. There will be a point when you will have clarity of what He or She is saying to you. Once this point is reached, there are no more excuses such as I "can't do it" because you know exactly what you need to do. This is a double-edged sword. I however feel that if you listen to this inner voice that you develop, you will not be disappointed with how your life turns out. Believe me, although it is scary at times, life becomes amazing and fulfilling the longer you listen, the greater the changes in your life.

Living a life true to yourself is the most important step in protecting yourself. The moment you step out of alignment and what your purpose is, is the moment you become a slave. It is the moment that you become unhappy with yourself. When you do what you know is best for you and for those around you by living in alignment, you are always happy with yourself. This happiness comes from your heart and is not dependent on outside factors. If you are completely out of alignment and unhappy this draws like energies or energies that feed on the depression frequency, namely, astral parasites. The happier you are with yourself and the more you love yourself, the more impenetrable are your psychic barriers for these low frequency astral parasites.

Living in alignment is an everyday process. At times your purpose may change or transition into new more aligned purposes. The key thing to realize is that your purpose and hearts desires change according to what the need is for you and for those around you. This happens because you are one-hundred percent Universe and one-hundred percent Individual at the same time when you are in alignment.

Realizing this specific point at all times will keep you centered everyday of your life. A specific mantra or chant for you to use in order to really tap into this belief or in actuality, this reality, is as follows.

"*I am Free of the Energy Extraction Matrix, I am one-hundred percent Universe and one-hundred percent Individual, I am the only god that is!*"

A good time to state this mantra is during meditation or at bedtime before falling asleep. Expect powerful results if you give it due attention. Say it over and over in your head or out loud until you fall asleep.

This is one way of moving your energies into alignment. Other ways of doing so are presented throughout the pages ahead.

At first glance it may appear to be blasphemous to say that you are the "only god that is," but let me be clear and say that if you are not okay with owning your own divinity and personal power, then Soul healing and Retrieval is not for you. If you are happy to embrace personal power and happiness without enslavement of your mind and energy to outside influence then by all means…read on and do what is written here.

The moment you pray to a God that you believe is separate from you, and in total authority over you, is the moment that you deny your Inter-Dimensional-Self. It is this moment that you accept the created reality of enslavement to beings that are less divine than yourself. Understand that Goddess/God/Universe are all within you. Not just within you but they are you. You are the same consciousness separated by layers and layers of time and space. Understand? When time, matter and space are completely disassembled then what is left…only you.

The point that you realize this Self-Awareness is the moment you are truly a God. It is what I would describe as a Dark-Enlightenment. Why do I call it "Dark-Enlightenment" you ask? Because it is not something that you can find or experience by submission to external Powers or Authorities. You are not a slave…you must be free to do what you love and seek the knowledge you need in order to have this Enlightenment.

This is the Essence of the Left-Hand-Path and the essence of alignment with your I.D.S. This book is Left-Hand-Path Magick, make no mistake. If you thought Left-Hand-Path Magick was or is something evil and to be feared then you have been misinformed. It is in actuality neither good nor evil. Some practitioners are evil yes, but this is true for those who practice Right-Hand-Path Magick as well. How many millions have been slaughtered in the name of Christianity?

Chapter 5
Magickal Practice Basics

This chapter will outline how to do basic, modern ritual Magick and provide basic Rites, Tools, groundwork for successful Magickal Practice that will be required for the rest of the work in this book. You may know how to do Magick and have your own tools already, if so, you may skip through this chapter.

I am writing this chapter based on experience and knowledge developed through practice. It is my own take on the basics of how to do Magick. It is not from another author's work and I will indicate if I barrow from other books. I do borrow some technique from S. Connolly's works and I did learn some of the general info from other books in the beginning. My goal is to keep things simple and up front. I want you to be able to do Magick without feeling overwhelmed.

Half the things you need to know for successful Magick are the Energy-Management skills we went over earlier. If you can successfully do them, then Real Magick is within your grasp and skill set already. You can do this without fear or doubt. I will guide you step by step. Do what I say one thing at a time with patience and consistency and you will be a good Magickian, Witch, Sorceress/Sorcerer or whatever your path may be. Magick is not exclusive to only one path. It is practice that links all of our paths together in one way or another.

Be sure that you know Energy Management well before continuing into this chapter. These are once again, skills needed to do Magick.

Magickal Practice Basics Part One
Ritual tools

The tools needed for Magick are all within you in my opinion, but Magickal practice is greatly enhanced by external tools consecrated for practice such as an Athame (pronounced Ah-them-ay), Altar, Pentacle, Wand, and Chalice for example. More important than any tool for Magick is an appropriate space for conducting meditation and ritual practice.

A sacred space is the cornerstone and foundation for successful Magick. It is what really matters for this work. If you live alone, you may use your bedroom for this purpose if no other space is available, but proper banishing is even more important if you are using such a personal space.

I will outline a simple banishing rite for your use later in Chapter Six. It is very important to know how to banish and to do it before and after most rites.

If you cannot get any of the ritual tools that I outline ahead, then at the very least have the right space. It can be any room that does not have people (other than yourself) and activity in it on a regular basis. It needs to be a place where you will not be disturbed unless it is an absolute emergency. If you live in an area that has space outside where you may go to do Magick then this is a good idea as well.

Additionally, clearing the space is also essential for successful Magick. If the space is loaded with unwanted entities and influences etc. then your Magick will undoubtedly be interfered with and fail to deliver results.

I will outline a very basic, but effective means of clearing the space you intend to use for your Magickal Practice. You will need a glass or bowl of clean water mixed with salt. This particular clearing Rite is a method I received from the Greek/Roman Witch Goddess, Hecate. It is an easy effective clearing method that will do an effective job at getting your space ready. It may be used throughout your whole living space if desired or any space that needs a good cleanse.

Simple Clearing Rite

Step One:
Fill a glass or bowl half full of clean, fresh water. Stir in a couple teaspoons of salt. Now holding the cup or bowl in the left hand, place your index finger and middle finger of your other hand together into the bowl, barely touching the water.

Step Two:
Say the words three times in a vibrating voice, "Hecate (Hek-Ka-Tay) Hah-Vee-Eh-Ah". The consecration word is spelt phonetically so you can pronounce it easier. As you are saying the word feel the buzzing energy channel through your fingers into the cup or bowl. Visualize the water within the vessel glowing with bright white clearing energy.

Step Three:
Now holding the vessel in your left hand, walk around your space in a clockwise circle from one side to the other while using your right hand to dip fingertips (index and middle fingers) into the water, point to the above and say "as above" now point to the below with the same hand and say "so below". Re-dip fingers and then repeat all around the space visualizing it becoming white and clear of all negative energies.

And… your space is cleared. Simple enough right? Do not forget to thank Hecate after the clearing is completed ok. A more potent and full clearing Ritual will be provided later on.

Basic Ritual Tools In Order Of Importance

1. Athame

The Athame (pronounced Ath-em-ay) is the tool that is symbolic of the Air element. It is a short dagger or knife that is usually no longer than eight inches and that traditionally has a black hilt. One places the Athame on the Eastern quarter of the Altar or area you are using as an altar.

If you do not have an altar yet then place your tools on top of a neat, clean area on the floor if you must. You may lay a black piece of fabric or folded sheet on the floor/ground as a altar area. If outdoors use a stone or tree stump as an Altar if you want.

Because it is a mainly a tool to stimulate your unconscious mind, it does not need to be sharp. (If you had a sharp knife for cutting things it would be a separate tool. Some use an additional separate knife for bloodletting. If you were to do this as part of a rite, it would be your blood only. Also, it would be cleanly done for manifestation purposes not as a sacrifice, but sometimes as an offering/gift. I will explain more about this later.) The reason it is the first tool you should acquire and consecrate is that it is used for banishing rites, casting a Magick Circle, and evocations. Much of the most important Magick is done with an Athame I feel. I feel is a tool for directing your intent.

The Athame is used instead of your index finger and middle finger (which are used if you do not have an Athame) in these operations and more.

You can find an Athame in most Pagan or New Age shops or through online shopping. I recommend that you buy one with a wooden hilt because you may want to inscribe Runes, Theban script or even sigils of your making to give the Athame special Magickal properties or meaning for you as a Witch or Magickian.

The Athame must be consecrated before use. The way I choose to consecrate ritual implements or tools does not require using said tools. It only requires the use of some sage leaves or sticks (any smudging or clearing herb/wood/resin will do), a bowl of consecrated water (As described in the Rite to cleanse space.), a candle, and some salt.

If for some reason you are in a hurry and do not have time to consecrate your Athame, you may use a feather in its place. A feather works best if you ask the Goddess or the Universe for one and then walk around areas where you live that have wildlife. You should have no problem finding a feather somewhere on the ground depending on where you live. If you find one be sure to clean it when you get inside. They can have mites or other small insects on them.

A Raven or Crow feather works best for any kind of Magickal practice whether they are consecrated or not because these birds are very Magickal creatures by themselves. Although feathers are ok to use without consecration you should still smudge the item and ask the Goddess to bless it for its use in your Magick.

2. Pentacle

The Pentacle is the ritual tool symbolic of the Earth element. It is placed on the altar on the Northern quarter. The pentacle is a disc shaped tool preferably made of copper or wood, but you may use one that you buy from a New Age or Pagan shop. It is essentially a pentagram with a circle around its outer perimeter. It does not need to be fancy and decorated with sigils or symbols, but later when you are more experienced you may feel inclined to do so. For now keep it simple and use it as the basic Earth element Magickal tool.

The pentacle in my experience is mostly used as a stimulus for the unconscious mind. One does not pick it up and use it very often in Magick. I have not had much need to do this personally anyway, but use your intuition about this in your Magick. If you feel like you need to use it, then do so. For me though when I use a Pentacle in ritual it is usually traced with my Athame or hand and visualized. This is done to bring in or banish elemental energies or other forces.

I prefer to keep my pentacle at an inverse position on the altar. Meaning the top point pointing downward and the two lower points pointed upward. I do this as a reminder of my Left-Hand-Path orientation and so the spirits present know my orientation. It is up to you to position your pentacle in a position that feels comfortable for you.

If you need a pentacle or something symbolic of the Earth element in an emergency or to use until you consecrate one, then use a small bowl of coarse salt or even a bowl of soil.

3. Wand

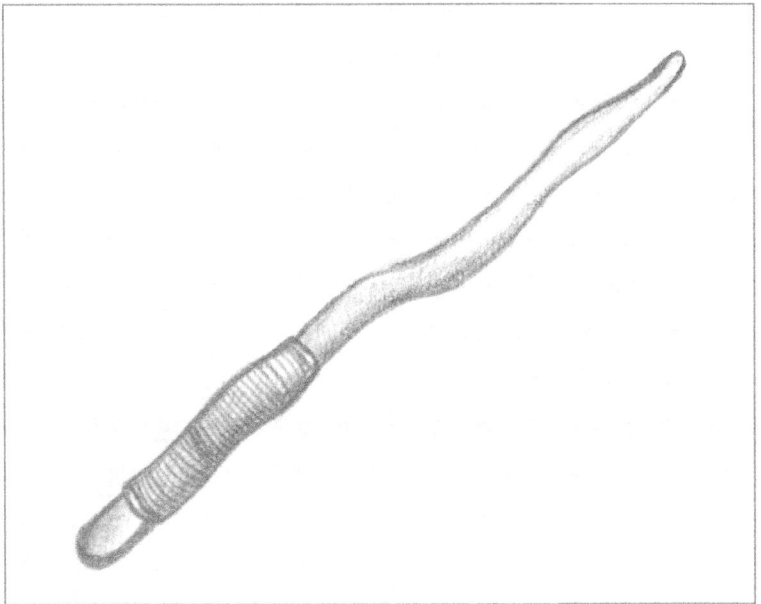

The Wand is symbolic of the Masculine Fire Element and it is made of out of wood, preferably Willow wood. It can be made from other types of wood. The Wand is usually at least the length of your forearm and no longer than the length of your outstretched hand and forearm combined. The Wand is an extension of your Magickal Will. It is used to direct energies and to call upon spiritual/energetic forces. It is similar in some respects to the Athame in how it is used. For example, like the Athame it can be used in evocation or summoning spirits.

The Wand is placed on the alter in the Southern position or in the direction that you associate with the Fire Element in your Magickal Practice.

I recommend carving your own Wand from a tree branch that is not alive rather than taking it from a living tree branch if you choose to carve your own out of wood. There are other options like purchasing a wand that is already carved or made of another quality material that calls to you.

If you cannot make or consecrate a Wand right away, but you need to do some Magick; you may use a lit candle as a symbol of Fire. Another option if you cannot use open flame is to use a flameless tea light. It is a candle that uses a light-bulb that flickers instead of flame.

4. Chalice

The Chalice is symbolic of the Feminine Water Element and is traditionally made of silver or silver like material. It is used to hold wine or other sacred fluid during a ritual. The cup or Chalice is very important to have on the Altar because it is symbolic of the Dark Feminine or creative energies of the Goddess, or the Primal Void (Womb of The Dragon).

Often during a Rite or Ritual one will imbibe the Fluid in chalice with an intention and then drink of the fluid in order to imbibe themselves with the same intention/energy.

The chalice will usually be purchased not carved by the Magickian/Witch and then consecrated. It should be placed on the Western portion of the Altar.

If you are in a rush and do not have time to consecrate a chalice until later then use a seashell as a symbol of the Goddess energy and Water Element. Remember to ask the Goddess or the Universe to bless the shell for use in your Magick however.

5. Altar

The Altar is symbolic of the foundations of the Earth plane that you live in/on...if the Earth were *flat* then think of the Altar as a miniature version of the Earth. It should be round. A flat, round stucture...(hint), but a also a square table is acceptable. I personally recommend placing a Pyramid shaped stone or other material that you have available in the center of your Altar. So a round table is what you should buy or make. It does not matter too much what kind of wood it is made out of, but I do not recommend plastic or some other cheap material. It needs to be metal or wood. The Altar may be placed in the Northern portion of your space or chamber/temple of practice. In the center or in the West is also acceptable. I recommend placing your Altar in the North for good results in any kind of Magickical Practice.

If you do not have an Altar table then fold a black sheet or piece of fabric into a square shape and place it on the floor in your space as an Altar.

Do not worry about consecrating the Altar itself. Just make sure you clear it with the clearing water used to clear your space.

To set up your Altar place a black piece of fabric over it evenly so that it looks neat and the same length on the sides. If the surface of your Altar is acceptable as is, then you may place your Magickal tools directly on it along with other items that you would like to use as Magickal objects, e.g. crystals, stones, incense burners, photos or art of the spirits that you choose to work with etc.

If you have a temple or space that you will be using on a regular basis then I urge you to place clear or smoky quartz in each corner of the space to keep it clear of negativity. Charge and clear the quartz in the sun on a window sill for at least a day's time and repeat as needed.

Consecration Of Your Tools

This is where I explain how to consecrate the tools you have made/acquired. Once these tools are consecrated no one but you may use them. You cannot deconsecrate them after it is done. If you have a tool that is no longer needed or wanted then you may burry it deep in the Earth where it will not be disturbed. The Earth will reabsorb it.

Here I will outline a general Consecration Rite that will utilize the Witchcraft currents of Hecate. This short consecration Rite will be used on all of the basic tools I have mentioned above. I will indicate any changes or differences in the Rite for each tool. You may look elsewhere for Consecration Rites that are more specific if you desire or if you do not want to work with the energies of the Goddess Hecate for whatever reason.

I have found Hecate to be amicable and helpful. Treat her with respect and she will do the same for you.

You may perform this Rite one time, but repeat the rite if you feel like your tools have lost their charge. This is unlikely, but it can happen. Usually the tools will become more powerful the more you use them in Magickal Practice.

The Consecration Rite requires the use of a Magick Circle and Banishing Rite. I have provided both Rites in Chapter Six for your use. It is best to memorize them, but if you only memorize one of them, then memorize the Banishing Rite called *The Cleansing Rite Of The Goddess*.

The Banishing Rite is important to know in order to feel secure during ritual practice if something goes awry. It is good to have on hand at all times. By "on hand" I mean known by heart. However, this is not a requirement until you get to the Advanced Magickal Practice in Chapter Eight.

Set up your altar with your Magickal Tools neatly placed on its front, facing you, within your immediate reach. Have one white candle, one bowl of consecration water, i.e. regular water mixed with some salt then consecrated with the words ("Heh-Kah-Tee Hah-Vee-Eh-Ah"), and some consecration incense -Dragon's blood resin, or Frankincense resin work great, but if you cannot get either of these, stick or cone incense is acceptable.

The Rite Of Consecration

Step One:
After your Altar is setup and everything is in place for the Rite you may use the Cleansing Rite of The Goddess (As described in Chapter Seven.) to clear your space in preparation.

Step Two:
Light the incense and the candle placed upon the Altar then cast the Circle Of Heka as described in Chapter Six of this book.

Step Three:
Now thank the Spirits present for supporting you in the consecration process, and at this you will call Hecate into your space by chanting times three **"Gahee-hah-kwee-ooae-Vee!!"** Feel her presence in the chamber and thank her for her participation in the Rite as well. Make sure your intention is clear in your mind and known to the spirits in your space. Remember your intention of clearing and dedicating your Ritual Tools for your Magick throughout the Rite.

Step Four:
Then begin by dipping your index finger and thumb in the consecration water and sprinkling it on the Tools in front of you (only a couple drops are needed) as you chant/intone the word of consecration three times **"Kee-ah-Zie-eeduh-ee-eh"**.

Step Five:
Now take each Ritual Tool and quickly (So they do not burn.) pass them through the candle flame. As you do so have the intention of purification by fire, see light of the flame clearing the Tools. Again intone the word three times as you do so. You can intone three times per Tool if you desire but it is not necessary.

Step Six:
Now pass the Tools through the smoke of the incense while you chant the word once again. See and feel the smoke clearing and dedicating the Tools to your Magickal Practice…remember your intention.

Step Seven:
When you are finished with the above steps, thank the Spirits present one at a time and bid them farewell.
If you would like to express greater gratitude and reflect on this feeling of gratitude toward spirit then say ***"Buh-Cuh-Huh-Kuh-Hah-Fer-Veh-Kuh-Ree <u>Name of Spirit</u>"***

Step Eight:
Now you may close the Circle and Banish the space once again.

Some may feel this is an overly simplified consecration ritual, but I have found that using the right words and intention has a powerful effect, simple or not. If you feel that this is too simple for you, then by all means consecrate your Ritual Tools again later when you are a more experienced Magickian or Witch.

After the Rite is complete you may want to put your newly consecrated Ritual Tools in a safe place. It is recommended to wrap your Tools in a piece of silk fabric to protect them. I personally leave my tools on my Altar and cover the top of the Altar with a piece of red silk.

Chapter 6
Magickal Practice Basics Part Two

Here in this Chapter you will find two important Rites that are to be used almost always if you do Magick and even when you meditate. Those are the Banishing Rite and The Magick Circle. Some Witches or Magickians choose not to use Banishing Rites or Magick Circles, but as I have said in the past, it is very *important!* Especially if you are a beginner at doing Magick. Why? you may ask. Because spirit is all around us, some are enemies, some are friends, some are neither, but may choose to feed on the energies you are calling or even your life-force itself as is the case with Archonic parasites. Why risk getting toyed with by your enemies? Cast your Circle and Banish every time you do Magick.

The following Banishing Rite is called the Cleansing Rite Of The Goddess. It was written by the present author as are all the Rites in this book with the help of the various spirits mentioned in the Rites themselves. It is designed to go beyond just allowing a clearing of your space. It was written to clear your path and allow you to stay centered and focused in your daily life. It allows a person to have more needed clarity in their life and their Magickal Practice if used on a regular basis. It should be committed to memory for best results and for any emergency situation in which you need to banish with urgency.

The Rite utilizes the Inverse Banishing Pentagram which is traditionally used in Left-Hand-Path Magick. I have found it to be a very effective and positive symbol in my life despite the bad rap it may have in some circles. The Inverse Pentagram is not an evil symbol. It is a symbol of fierce defiance of convention, freedom and Magickal Will. It is a symbol that can connect you to your Inter-Dimensional-Self and keep you aligned with Him or Her.

In the Cleansing Rite Of The Goddess you will use your Athame in your dominant hand or your index and middle fingers together to trace the Inverse Pentagram in the air before you. You must visualize the symbol as if it were glowing in front of you after you trace it.

Make sure you take a deep breath before you trace each Inverse Pentagram (You will trace one at each Cardinal Direction.) Exhale as you trace, this will allow you to put your chi into the Rite and create a stronger effect.

The Cleansing Rite Of The Goddess

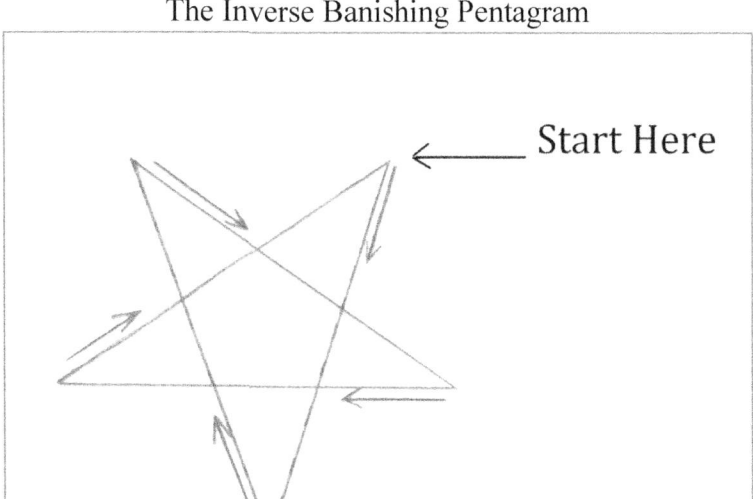

The Inverse Banishing Pentagram

Step One:
Face East with your Athame in your hand at the ready. Now trace the First Inverse Pentagram visualizing it glowing before you like a flaming neon sign. Let the color be whatever your imagination gravitates to. Now point to the center of this shining Pentagram with your Athame as you intone the words (Vibrate your voice like you were saying a chant.) " ***Zie-Tee-Ee-Ray*** " x3 then say ***"By the light of Isis, Guardian of the Land Of Khem, let my spirit, mind and body be defended from evil Will!!"***
See Isis descend from above with her scepter in hand, her wings fully outspread. She lands directly front of you and turns toward the East away from you warding all Evil from you and your space with her Magick, her wings and her scepter. Feel her fierce presence fully deflecting your enemies advance and bolts of lightning flash from the clouds above.

Step Two:
Now face the North and repeat the tracing of the Inverse Pentagram, point to the center and intone **"Vee-Dah-Ee-Tee-Fie-Ooae-Ee"** x3 then say **"Through the radiant essence of Hathor, may my spirit be uplifted and made whole!!"**
See a massive blue and gray whirlwind of Hathor's power come rushing to you and encircle your aura. Her power uplifts you, removes negative energies, heals you and restores your aura.

Step Three:
Now face the West and repeat the tracing of the Inverse Pentagram and Point to the Center once again, then intone **"Gahee-Hah-Kwee-Ooae-Vee"** x3 then say **"By the Infernal Powers of Hecate and The Primal Void of The Dragon, let my being cleansed and empowered!!"**
Envision Hecate coming forth from the Abyss. She is dressed in traditional Greek garments and has pale skin with jet black hair. She cuts all negative bindings from you and frees you from heavy emotional burdens. See her four Black Jaguars (Panthers) surround you and free you of all fears and anxieties.

Step Four:
Now face the South and trace the Inverse Pentagram once again, pointing to the center intone **"Eh-Buh-Fie-Dumah-Fay"** x3 then say **"By the Will of Astarte, may my path be clear and my vision be sure!!"**
See Astarte come from the South in a fiery flash of light. Take a moment to allow her to impart to you her blessings and powers of clarity. She will often reveal obstacles and enemies in your path.

Step Five:
Stand facing the East with arms raised out from your sides facing North and South say **"Before me Auset-Sekhmet! Behind me Babalon-Hecate! At my right Venus-Inanna!! At my left Het-Heru-Isis!! For about me shines the Pentagram and within me burns the heart the Goddess for all time!!"**

The next Rite you will learn is called The Circle Of Heka, it is a Magick Circle received from The Neteru or Egyptian Gods and Azazel, the Daemon King. It is a very useful Magick Circle for beginners and advanced Magickians/Witches alike. It harnesses the powers of the White Sun (The sun in the sky you see daily.) and powers of the Black Sun. Connecting with these bodies/spheres gives you tremendous manifestation potential. They are both loaded with Chi that will empower your Rites and Rituals.

Azazel and Set are the Gatekeepers of the Black Sun and Horus and Ra are the Gatekeepers of the White Sun when using this circle. The Black Sun is not some symbolic etheric thing that does not exist in the physical world. I believe that it is a literal Sun in the Lower-world. Open your mind's eye and look to the North. There you will see the vortex at the center of the Earth Plane, the Gate to the Lower-world. The more you claim the lost parts of your spirit with this book the more you will see and Understand that the world we live in is a Matrix of our own creation and we have fallen asleep and lost pieces of ourselves within it. We have unknowingly surrendered our sovereignty to beings that use us for an energy snack.

Trust me and use this Circle for your Magickal Practice. The Words the Circle uses are not English, nor are they necessarily translatable. They are primal Words of Power that stimulate your subconscious mind. Intone the Words of Power to Invoke Each Spirit of the Circle Of Heka as if you were in a Temple Chanting/Singing a song of praise to the God or Goddess. You are not worshiping these Powers, you are paying respect to them. They do not need you to worship them. They want you to realize your own potential and Godhood status as bearers of the Black Flame.

The Black Flame is the realization and acknowledgement of your own divinity and sovereignty. It is the spark or source of your consciousness. You are God and you are Individual. This is the fundamental truth of what the Black Flame is. It is the realization of your Magickal Will to change your world into what you want it to be. It is the Will to be a creator, not a victim of circumstance. Your Will is free and shall not be taken from you any longer.

The Circle of Heka (Magick)

Begin by facing the North, right hand raised with index finger and middle finger together pointing (if you have a consecrated Athame, then use it instead of your hand) in the air, intone…

SET! HKYK HKYK WHKAM KUA SET!!!
Pronunciation: Suh-Etah Huh-Kuh-Yeh-Kuh Huh-Kuh-Yeh-Kuh Wuh-Huh-Kuh-Ah-Muh Kuh-ooahh Suh-Etah!!!

Visualize SET coming forth from the North into the chamber or sacred space you are using. His eyes glow with bluish white light, his head is all black, with an elongated nose and jaw, his ears are large and pointed on the top of his head. He is holding the Uas (Was) Scepter, a symbol of might and power. As he approaches, you sense his aura of unbound chaos….you know he has the power to destroy or create. His body adorned in Egyptian ornaments is muscular and lean, emanating masculinity.

Now turn and face the West. Pointing your Athame or two fingers toward the West, intone…

Ra! LStfD-I-Lf Ra!!!
Pronunciation: Reeah! Luh-Suh-Tah-Fuh-JEh eye Luh-fuh Reeah!!!

See Ra come forth from the West into your space. He is a Solar God who often appears with a hawk's head and sometimes with a human head. He wears the Sun-disc upon his head encircled by a cobra and holds an Ankh in his hand. As he approaches you feel his presence of illumination, protection and healing encircle your being. Sometimes he appears as a setting sun in the distance.

Now face the Southern point of your space. As before, hand or Athame in the air before you pointed in the Southern direction, intone…

Azazel! gAz razDgRf AfBDzf f LD Azazel!!!
Pronunciation: Azazel! Guh-Ah-Zuh Reeuh-zuh-Jeh-guh-ree-fuh Ah-fuh-Buh-Jeh-zuh-fuh fuh Luhjeh Azazel!!!

See Azazel (a horned God) come forth from the South. He holds his head high and walks with a great sense of pride that is palpable. Sometimes he comes as a large Crow or Raven. His face will often appear goat-like and his horns are those of a Ram.

Now Turning to the Eastern Cardinal Point, direct the Athame in the air before you and intone…

Horus! Sftb I L-I-gHgLf Horus!!!
Pronunciation: Huh-oh-reeoo-suh Suh-fuh-tuh-buh eye Luh-eye-guhHuh-guh-Luh-fuh Huh-oh-reeoo-suh

See and feel the presence of the Neter Horus as he approaches or appears from the East. He appears as a Falcon headed man wearing the Crowns of Upper and Lower Egypt. Sometimes he appear as a rising sun. His presence feels vitalizing and powerful. He at times is accompanied by a lion who is fierce, leaping and bounding around him.

When your spell-work or Ritual is complete close the Circle of Heka by saying to each Neter and Azazel…

Thank you (Name of Spirit) and farewell, go in peace.

Chapter 7
Advanced Preliminary Rites Of Soul Retrieval

In this chapter I will teach you step by step how to use Magickal Practice to destroy the mind control Matrix or Energy Extraction Matrix that you may currently be a slave to. I have used these Rites that I will show you on myself with great and empowering results. I know after doing these Rites exactly where I will go when this body dies, or rather when I choose to release this vehicle that I now inhabit. We can choose when we want to leave and we can choose where we want to go when we "die" contrary to the programming and fear driven mind control enslavement of modern society.

Let me explain in a little bit more detail. We are creators…we have total free Will. Now, we may have made some agreements that our Inter-Dimensional-Self may not want to alter, but there is a lot of wiggle room. My life was supposed to be one of tragedy and learning to suffer the feeling of loss and powerlessness. Well after the tragedy chapter of my life was over by my own Will, I willed even greater changes and healing for myself than was ever expected for me. I Willed all the victimhood of my tragic early life into oblivion. I chose to fight and change the course of my life. I felt the tremendous power within me. I knew that no one had power over me.

No God and no Man has ultimate power over me, they may have temporary power, but that is just that "temporary". I used the vehicle of Magickal Practice to enforce my Will for myself. I cut myself free of the Lie. The Lie in this context is what I had been taught by the world around me from birth. I realized that what I knew and saw with my own sight was the truth not what others told me; they were just repeating what they were told by others and so on down the line.

The tools of discipline and Magickal Practice are what helped me to become who I am, despite all the odds against me. This can be true for you as well. Follow these Rites and expect a dramatic change of vantage point in your life. See things as they are. Do not stick your head in the sands of illusion any longer. Why should you be a Dog? Why should you be what everyone else thinks is "normal"…you know what, no one is normal if you ask me.

What's normal about automatons that kneel to the T.V. and to the fake leaders of this world? The T.V. and the "authorities" are not your leaders…stop listening to them and instantly *You* become your leader. Stop watching the filtered, altered news stories of which at least fifty percent, is not even true.

The Rites ahead will cause you to change. You will feel different and see things as they are. You may think at times that you are going insane or that you are just imagining things. This is not the case. You must do them with sincerity and wholehearted intention if you want results though.

The use of your blood in Magick

This I think is a touchy subject for some, but I must tackle it here and inform you of some facts about using blood that you may not know. If you are new to Magick then you are more than likely afraid to have anything to do with it, do to lies and programming of the false leaders of this Matrix. You are constantly bombarded with the idea that using blood in Magick is "evil" and for evil Sorcerers only. Well allow me to have the honor of telling you the truth, that this is all a pile of steamy Bullshit!

Blood is your vital energy in a physical form which has your specific energy signature attached to every single little cell. It is your essence and a very potent Magickal tool for various reasons.

It allows you to program your reality by giving a few drops toward your intention during a Rite or Ritual.

All that is required from you is a couple drops for most Rites. No, you do not need to slice your hand or wrist and leave scars all over. It is easy and painless to use a diabetes test lancet to extract a few drops of blood and no one will admit you to psychiatric facility for being a danger to yourself this way.

If you really are against using blood because of whatever reason, you may use sexual fluids in its place, but I personally think this route is messy and requires more skill on the part of the Magickian to do correctly. Although, it is a more powerful source of your energy, because of the orgasm itself, it also costs you more in vital energy to use.

Women may use menstrual blood if desired for their Magick, but once again be careful because this proves to be a more powerful source or so I have heard. Obviously I have no personal experience with this being a Male Witch.

Again your blood is not evil. Your blood is yours to do with as you please. You are willing to give pints of your vital blood energy to blood drive organizations, so how is it wrong or evil to use your blood to improve your life through Magickal Practice. It is not wrong to use this Magickal tool. It is your birthright as a sovereign creator being.

Do not be fooled by lying shit bag fake leaders. Sorry to be so vulgar, but I have had enough lies shoveled down my throat to last me a lifetime. I say, no more lies for me! I do what works and what is right for my soul, for my freedom and personal power to be maximized. Do not be relegated to mediocre existence because you have been brainwashed into fearing the gods of enslavement, the gods that demand you suffer at their feet while they drain you of all your pride, joy, and life-force until you become a dried-up, worthless bag of depressed bones waiting to get recycled by the Matrix. What comes next after your death? You repeat the cycle of slavery without your memory of your previous incarnation as if your reason to exist is to be a battery of energy that is consumed.

Do you want that? Do you want to come back here and get lied to again and be a *victim* again? I personally do not like it one bit, and I for one will give some blood to bring forth my Will in this world in a heartbeat if it means breaking out of the cage of mind control. You will know what I mean when you open your eyes and see this place for what it is.

The Use of Baneful or Cursing Magick

Do not be stubborn and think love and light are all you need to break out of the mind Matrix. The Rites that follow will require you to be a violent in your intent. They require you to TAKE back what is yours! This is not going to happen if you pussyfoot through this book. I will ask you to curse your true enemies, to weaken their hold on you and break the illusion filters that they hide behind. They are there laughing at you, and eating your vital energy on a daily basis. You should be angry! You should take back your energies, every bit they ever stole from you. It does not belong to them! Take it back, curse them!! You are not harming some innocent person or elemental here. If you have not guessed, I am talking about the major astral parasites known as Archons.

The Rites ahead require you to destroy them with all your powers and intentions. This will loosen their hold over you long enough for you to wake up. Then we will move into The Rites of actual Soul Retrieval by which you will claim lost knowledge and lost parts of your Soul. No longer will you be a shattered spiritual mess of missing pieces and confusion. You will know your hearts desires and become the only God that is. This is to say that you Worship no fake authorities…and all authorities that want you to grovel at their feet are weak, insecure beings, let us be honest. Do not waste any more time. Cut the cords and be a free Spirit.

This process of Soul Retrieval requires a warrior's spirit, it is not for people are not ready for it. You must keep up the momentum of this work and do it step by step with only short breaks if needed. You cannot be squeamish about using Magick to harm your enemies if you want to get through this book. If you have a problem with cursing those who are destroying you, then you might as well put this book down and get on your "drone" knees where you belong!! I am saying these things bluntly only to get you fired up for this work. After all that is how they see you. You know that right? You are a drone to them. To the false leaders, the Archons, and the Controllers of this Matrix. The longer you let them fuck you up without consequences, the harder it will be for you to make the internal changes needed to fight back…wake up!!

The Curse Breaker Rite
(A Rite to Deflect/Remove all Curses, Hexes, and Bindings from you and your space)

This Rite is important to know and have on hand at all times during the Soul Retrieval process or the process of working through this book. This is because in performing cursing Magick there will often be cursing energy directed back at you. It will either come from the Curse energy you sent that was deflected or from a retaliation by one of the beings that you will need to curse in this work. And quite often these beings like to put binding Magick on people who try to break free of them.

I recommend performing the following curse breaker Rite whenever you get the feeling that something is off or just not right with your energy despite the Energy Management you perform daily. If you feel "off" it is usually a sure sign of either a curse or binding energy placed on you.

Personally I will usually see the sigil of Atum in my mind's eye as a warning from spirit that a Curse Breaker must be done. Rather than waiting until everything is set up I will usually begin chanting the Curse Breaker Word that Atum provides while I set up for the Rite or until I have the free time to do it. The Word of Power spelt phonetically is "Vey-Yeh-Hah-Suh-Ree-Bah-Hah-Veh". I always intone or chant the name Atum and then the Word of Power for maximum effect.

Preparation for the Rite

To do this Rite you will need all your consecrated Ritual Tools neatly in place on your Altar, one to three black candles and the Sigil of Atum and an unbinding glyph beneath it is needed and should be drawn in black ink on a round or oval piece of parchment or paper. An example of this will be provided ahead. If you cannot draw then photo copy the image or print it out if you are using a digital copy of this book. If you can draw the basic shapes then it is good enough and will still work well, as long as your intention is there while you draw the Sigil. You will also need a pyramid shaped stone on the center of your Altar. The stone may be made of Lapis-Lazuli, Malachite or even Obsidian for best results. You may make a pyramid out of cardboard an paint it a blue or green color. Size does not matter, but each side can be about three inches in length if you need a measurement to go by. An offering bowl is also needed for this rite. You can use any bowl as long as it is not plastic. It is best to buy a bowl specifically for offerings, but it is not a necessity until you have the means to do so. You will need a chair in order to be seated when called for during this short Rite also. Additionally you must have a clean, sterile means of extracting a few drops of your blood. I recommend a diabetes test lancet, sterile pin or needle.

Incense is not necessary, but I recommend it for this Rite, to show respect to Atum. Use Frankincense and Myrrh resin or incense sticks. The resin in obviously the better choice if you are aiming for quality, but it is not as easy to use.

If for some reason you cannot acquire the incense or you cannot burn candles where you are, then do not despair. These are all tools to help you achieve results, but the real power comes from you and your intention. I do suggest a blood offering to the spirits you will be working with at least, or in addition to the incense. If you cannot do incense, blood by itself is the greatest show of respect to Spirit that you can give anyway. They will not reject your gift to them if you are sincere and respectful. If you are in a place where you cannot use your blood, then sexual fluids are acceptable, when offered toward your intention correctly.

Checklist of materials
1. Consecrated Ritual Tools
2. Pyramid shaped stone placed on center of the Altar
3. Frankincense and Myrrh resin or incense sticks
4. Offering bowl
5. One to three black candles
6. Diabetes test lancet or sterilized needle/pin
7. Oval or round piece of parchment with name and Sigil of Atum on it and the Word of Power ***"Vey-YHSR-BH-Veh"*** written on it and the intention statement ***"It is My Will to Remove/Deflect all Curses, Hexes and Bindings from me and my space."*** written on the reverse side.

Sigil to be used

Atum
"Vey-YHSR-BH-Veh"

The Curse Breaker Rite step by step

Step One:
Place all the Tools and other items neatly on the Altar or Altar space on the floor, including the completed sigil/parchment which should be placed leaning against the pyramid stone facing you (You should be able to see it clearly). You may also want to have a clear quartz crystal in each corner of your space as well. Make sure you have a lighter and open a window because you will be burning the parchment during the Rite. You may take it outside and burn it if you prefer and then return to the circle. Have a chair ready so you can be seated comfortably when called for during the Rite. Light any candles you have set up in the space for lighting (Perhaps one in each Cardinal Direction of the space.) If you are using resin incense, light the charcoal tablet you are using now. Now use the Cleansing Rite Of The Goddess which you may want to have memorized by this point.

Step Two:
Cast the Circle Of Heka place incense on the charcoal (or light the stick incense) and light the black candle/candles on the Altar.

Step Three:
Now take the pin/needle/lancet and prick your finger and place a few drops of blood in the offering bowl and few more drops on the sigil of Atum. You may place some directly on the intention statement on the reverse side if desired. Return the parchment to the front of the Pyramid stone on the Altar where you can see it clearly. Begin chanting the name of Atum as you anoint the Sigil. Now sing/intone his Evokation chant over and over until you feel Atum's presence grow strong:
"Atum Sah-Gahee-Eh-Fee-Dee-Key--Yek-Eed-Eef-He-Eehag-Has"

Step Four:
Be seated and gaze at the Sigil of Atum as you continue to chant his name. Now Intone the following ***"Atum Vey-Yeh-Hah-Suh-Ree-Buh-Hah-Veh"*** as you continue to gaze at the Sigil. Repeat the intonation at least three times. Feel your Will being done.

Step Five:
Stand up and pick up the Sigil parchment. Look at the intention statement and read it out loud. Then light it on fire using the black candles and place it in the offering bowl to burn, or take it outside and burn it if you have to. Place the ashes in the earth or a plant pot filled with earth/soil kept in your space. I do this to ground and manifest any remaining energies in the ashes.

Step Six:
Return to your seat in the circle and meditate for about ten to fifteen minutes allowing the clearing to take full effect. Take note of the feelings of gratitude you have and send them to the Spirits who are helping you with this Rite.

Step Seven:
Now you may stand and thank all the Spirits present, one by one and close the Circle Of Heka by saying "thank you and farewell" to each Neteru (Egyptian God) and to Azazel the Daemon King as well.

Step Eight:
Perform the Cleansing Rite Of The Goddess once again and that is end of the Rite.

What to expect after the Rite

After the Rite is completed you will feel relief from depressing, heavy thoughts and energies bearing down on you. You will feel lighter and happier. You will feel well and protected. Doubts and fears start to clear up and you will have the strength to move forward in your life purpose without negative energies holding you back. The Rite should be done on a regular basis during this work and after the work any time you feel like it is needed. The time may come when you are powerful enough to clear your energy of curses without the Rite, but until then do not risk your health and well-being; perform the Rite and remember to be thankful for help from spirit.

The Rite Of Sovereignty
(A cursing of the False Light Beings and proclamation of your Sovereignty)

This Rite is intended to help you to once and for all break free of any Archonic or energy parasite influence and draining. It will cause you to see them clearly if you have psychic ability and from there you may have to do the Rite a couple times to make them think twice about approaching you again. Then as needed after that. You may also use The Cursing Words of Power that are provided ahead for maintenance as well. You do not need a Ritual setting to use the Words of Power provided in this book. They may be intoned at any time and any place. Ritual settings and intention obviously makes them more powerful though.

Preparation for the Rite

For this Rite you will need all of your usual consecrated Ritual Tools on your Altar and the pyramid stone in the center. You will also need some Dragon's Blood incense sticks or resin. The Resin is more complicated to use, but is preferred over the incense stick because it is usually much higher quality. One to three black candles should be used during the Rite. Also you will need an offering bowl. You will also need a diabetes test lancet or sterilized pin/needle for bloodletting and the appropriate sigil on a small round piece of parchment (paper) which will be displayed below.

Keep a positive and resolute mindset before, during and after the Rite. Do not let the Archons scare you and bully you with fear energy. They have no real power over you except what you allow. All that you have allowed them to do was through manipulation. Take back your power from them now!! They will fight it, but you will prevail if you have the right attitude.

Checklist of materials
1. Consecrated Ritual Tools
2. Pyramid shaped stone placed on center of the Altar
3. Dragon's Blood resin or incense sticks
4. Offering bowl
5. One to three black candles
6. Diabetes test lancet or sterilized needle/pin
7. Oval shaped parchment with Sigils of Set and Seker and the Words of Power spelt phonetically, ***"Jeh-Kuh-Guh-Yeh-Kha-Jeh-Hah, and Yeh-Huh-Yeh-Huh-Ah-Veh-Vey"*** on front and the following intention written on the reverse side-***"It is my Will to Curse & Destroy All Archonic, Reptilian & Astral Parasites who have been feeding on me, draining me, controlling, deceiving and manipulating me!! So be it!!!***

Sigils to be used on parchment

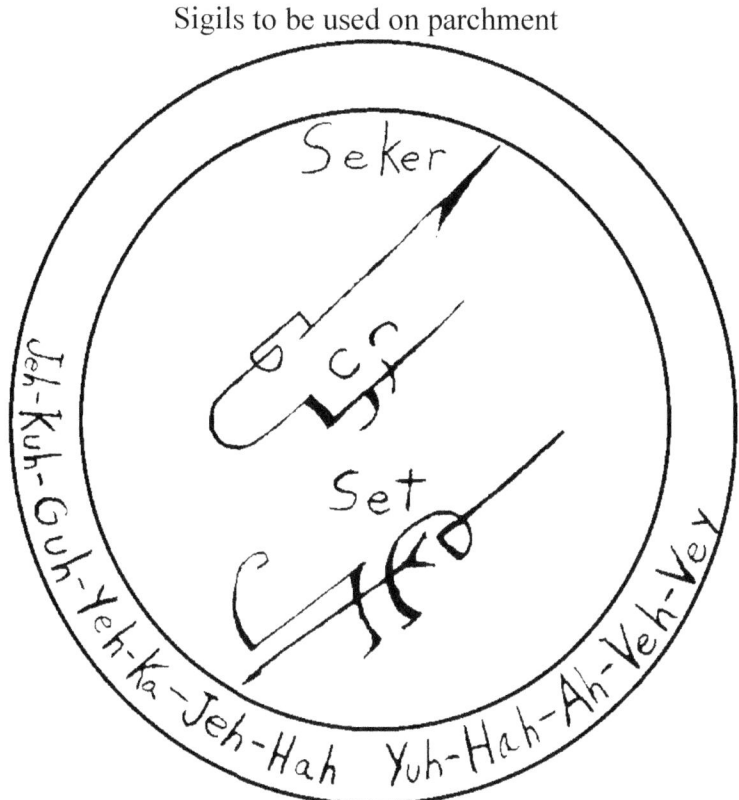

Jeh-Kuh-Guh-Yeh-Kha-Jeh-Hah
Yuh-Hah-Yah-Hah-Ah-Veh-Vey

The Rite of Sovereignty step by step

Step One:
As before in the Curse Breaker Rite, place all the Tools and other items neatly on the Altar or Altar space on the floor, including the completed sigil/parchment which should be placed leaning against the pyramid stone facing you (You should be able to see it clearly). You may also want to have a clear quarts in each corner of your space as well. Make sure you have a lighter and open a window because you will be burning the parchment during the Rite once again. Light any candles you have set up in the space for lighting (One in each Cardinal Direction of the space.) If you are using resin incense, light the charcoal tablet you are using now. Now use the Cleansing Rite Of The Goddess which you must have memorized by now.

Step Two:
Cast the Circle Of Heka place incense on charcoal (or light the stick incense) and light the black candle/candles on the Altar.

Step Three:
Now take the pin/needle/lancet and prick your finger and place a few drops of blood in the offering bowl and few more drops on the sigils of Seker and Set. You may place some directly on the intention statement on the reverse side if desired. Return parchment to the front of the Pyramid stone on the Altar where you can see it clearly. Begin chanting the names of Seker and Set, then intone/sing the Chants of Evokation for them until their presence grows strong:
For Seker-*"Wee-Ree-ah-Dew-Cuh-Eh-Ah-Luh-Dah-Dah--Had-Had-Hul-Ha-He-Huc-Wed-Ha-eer-Eew"*
For Set-*"Dee-Eff-Gahee--Ray-Eh-Sah-Ohay--Dew-Vey--Yev-Wed--Ayoh-Has-He-Yar--Eehag-Feh-eed"*

Step Four:
Be seated, the Altar should be in front of you. Begin chanting loudly with intention the Words of Power and the names of the Neteru (Egyptian Gods) you are working with. Say ***"Seker Jeh-Kuh-Guh-Ah-Yeh-Jeh-Huh Set Yeh-Huh-Yeh-Huh-Ah-Veh-Vay"*** x3. You will have trouble speaking the words if you have Archons or Parasites trying to make you second guess yourself…be steady minded and resolute. Do not doubt yourself at any point during the Rite.

Step Five:
Now staying seated begin chanting the following Mantra with supreme confidence and focus.
"I proclaim my Sovereignty, I take back ALL of My Vital Energies that have been stolen from me through Deception & Draining!!"
Continue until you feel a change come over you, a breaking point. You should feel energized and powerful. It will take about five minutes of steady chanting.

Step Six:
Now stand up and pick up the parchment and read your intention statement out loud that is written on the reverse side. Then fold up the parchment and burn it in the offering bowl releasing your intention to the Universe. Now sit back down and meditate on gratitude for the gift of freedom that you are receiving.

Step Seven:
Be sure to thank Seker and Set, then close the Circle Of Heka with Gratitude to each Spirit present. Remember, gratitude is powerful. Now Banish using the Cleansing Rite Of The Goddess or your favorite Banishing Rite.

What To Expect After The Rite

Immediately after and even during the Rite you will feel a change in your energy and your thinking, especially your thinking. You will find it much easier to stay positive, happy and avoid ruminating on issues that do not matter. You may feel heat building in your Chi centers as you receive the energies that were drained from you over time.

You will more than likely experience some intense dreams. I dreamed about spinal implant drone Archons being pulled out of my spinal cord and nervous system and then destroyed. You will most likely have similar dreams of these being removed from your astral body and from your home. You may experience a greater awareness of the presence of these Parasites as well. You may see them on others drinking their life force even while you are awake if your mind's eye is open.

You may have to repeat the Rite every couple months to stay cleared of parasites and at the first time you do it, you may have to repeat it the day after in order to cleanse yourself fully if you have a lot of parasite activity.

Remember not to feel guilty or worry about the morals or ethics of performing this Rite. More than likely it is just the Archons trying to regain a hold on you through your negative doubting ego mind. They can be sneaky and tricky. They strengthen your negative Ego in order to confuse you and prey on you again.

The Rite Of Implant Removal
(A removal of artificial implants and chakras)

The following Implant Removal Rite should only be done if and when you are ready for it. Chakra removal is still a relatively new concept and practice. It is not something that should be done by people who rely only on the concept of chakras to balance themselves.

I personally found it very liberating to never have to "balance my chakras" ever again!! What a relief to be free from the repetitive, never ending process of "balancing chakras". It felt like slavery to have to balance them every single day if you ask me.

I truly believe that you will be drawn to chakra removal at some point during your spiritual growth if you are not already. I worked on my chakras for over a decade and then one day my spirit guide lead me to remove them and I never looked back. I feel great everyday and I meditate on my organic Chi Centers. I never worry about blockages in my energy system because it flows freely now.

I would like to let my sister Sara, speak about Chakra removal in greater depth at this point in order for you to hear it from another person's perspective other than my own.

Sara Petrucelly On Chakra Removal

Why should you remove your chakras?

When you get to the point when you are centered and balanced. Your chakras are perfectly envisioned as swirling light energy as you have been taught in so many Yoga books and even YouTube videos. You do your morning Chakra adjustments and by nighttime they are out of whack again! So needy!!! So, you start another day over and over with same visualizations or maybe you try new ones, but they yield the same results, you stop growing spiritually and your energy level stops increasing. This may be the time to look into removing the chains that are your "Chakras". Expand your energy. You are ready! However, if you are not drawn to this idea, do not do it.

Energy Parasites

As an intuitive Empath, Reiki practitioner and Medium, I have been taught things from spirit concerning the Chakras and astral beings. Your Chakras are a huge weakness when it comes to the astral energy beings. They are around us every day, lurking… feeding from our aura. Sounds like a science fiction film I know. Have you ever woken from a slumber to see the faint outlines of spider like creatures before they fade away? They can be big or small, some crawl and some float above you. This is not your eyes playing tricks. These are astral vampires who feed off our energy systems. I believe our energy is too powerful for them to feed off when not held in the compartments of the Chakras. The Chakras weaken our energy system enough and put energy in "Tupperware" like containers for these entities. I myself on my spiritual journey began seeing these upon waking up from naps during the day as they are hard to see in the dark. I saw them on such an often occasion that I Googled "Seeing spiders when waking up." …what I found was overwhelming. Thousands of people were experiencing the exact same thing I was, but dismissed it as a trick of the eyes or a "medical condition." I meditated on it, asked for guidance. I continued opening my mind and pineal gland. The answer came to me. There are many names for these beings and they have been recorded about throughout history including in the Bible. Texts speak of low entities whom live in the astral realm feeding off energetic creatures such as ourselves. We must name them in order to destroy them. We must become aware of them.

We are most vulnerable when we are unguarded, unshielded, our vibration low…we are depressed, anxious, fearful or sick. It's very important to keep our vibration up and to use shielding techniques that work for you to avoid being drained constantly. Keep a healthy diet If possible because mind and body are one, and if or when you are led to it, remove those Chakras!

Chains for the Mind

Another great benefit I found to removing Chakras is the very idea we are taught, to have them balanced and clear constantly and that they are certain colors. This is no better than going to church and being told that you must be sin free or you go to hell. It is just as constricting to me and well…impossible. This kind of thinking is a prison for your mind. Set yourself free.

Debris

Finally, you are taught that the Chakras are swirling colors of energy, spinning like mini universes inside your energetic body. How I began to see these universes was more like swirling Tornados, sucking in junk from the outside world including the energy eating entities. Leaving your aura wide open and vulnerable like an open can of tuna attracting wild beasts to the feast. Meanwhile your Chakras are clogged by the end of the day by everyone else's energetic cyclone of garbage… sounds like fun. Again, even if you have Chakras please learn to shield more appropriately to avoid this. Shielding is so important! Especially if you are an Empath.

How I came to remove my Chakras and my questions about it

I made the decision to remove my Chakras after my brother Enoch and I had researched the idea and had been very drawn to it by spirit. My brother was the first to go through with it. I was reluctant at first, I had many questions. Will my third eye still be there? Will my crown Chakra still receive guidance? Will my root still ground me? The answers to these is yes, yes and more.

I finally went through with it after my brother successfully had gone a few months with no Chakras and noticed an incredible difference in his life, but that is his story to tell, I will go on with mine.

Medication free

I felt compelled to stop my anxiety and depression medicine and was successful. I was cured. Now this is not what I am recommending to people. Do not just go off your medication without doctor direction and approval. Before my spiritual changes and removing Chakras, I also changed to a vegetarian diet and avoided processed foods. This alone can assist with mental health issues. I am not saying I am now this perfectly emotionally balanced person and you will be to. I still have emotional issues to release from this life and others, anger to let go and love to learn. I find it easier to do this now without Chakras, however. I can work on myself without worrying about unblocking an annoying Chakra energy which was only a symptom of a deep-rooted problem to begin with.

Community Life

Being around others in the community is easier. I like I said, am an Empath and I find it hard to be around people at work or anyone who is very negative. I am still very sensitive and have my bad days, but for the most part I can deal with it. Negative energy from others is less entangled in my energy and easier to release once I am away from the negative environment. I feel I can understand people and their perspective better because I have a deeper connection to the "All are one" concept. I have more compassion and realize negative people just need healing. I take things less personally and see the big picture. So, these are only my experiences and everyone will have a different one. Chakra removal is not for everyone and not everyone will be accepting of such an idea. That is fine. I am only here to help those that it is right for and to share my thoughts and experiences with others. Thank you for taking the time to read this, I will end here and allow Enoch to continue.

Preparation For The Rite

In order to do this Rite Of Implant Removal you will need the same tools as were used in the previous Rite. A new sigil will be provided and different incense for this particular Rite will be used. Additionally I ask that you prepare yourself mentally for the inner changes that come with implant removal. It can significantly increase your psychic awareness in most people, because the implants themselves stunt energy and psychic channels that should normally be free flowing. Also be prepared to feel tired for a few days after the Rite, because of the magnitude of changes going on in your energy. You may want to take a few days off work and chill or at least take it easy.

By the time that you move forward with this step you must have control of your mind and emotions to the extent that you do not wish harm upon others for petty reasons. The reason for this requirement is that once you gain a certain amount of thought/psychic power you can accidently harm other people just by thinking it. For example, if I sit here and think about beating someone over the head with a baseball bat who is not psychically shielded, then it will likely cause them some real harm, e.g. they may get a bad headache. The same goes for any kind of hateful thoughts or directed emotions. If you have a hateful emotion and direct it at someone then it can harm them. So just be mindful of your thoughts and feelings…make sure that they match your intentions at all times.

The following Rite is for removing both chakra implants and other implants as well. You may want to do one, then the other if you feel that it will be too much at once. If so, alter the intention statement for the Rite accordingly.

The Major Chakras

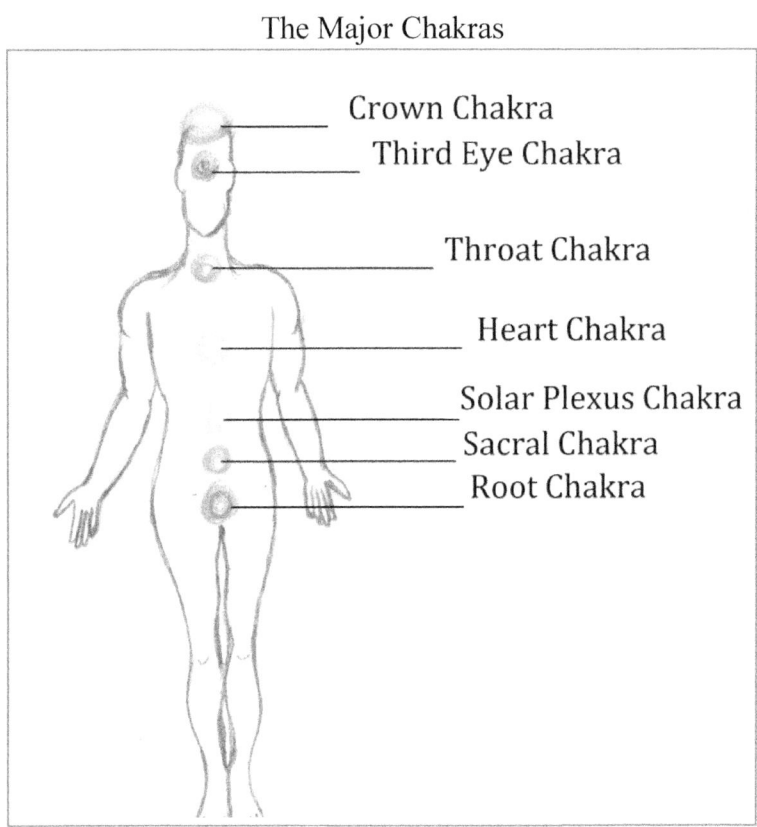

Checklist of materials
1. Consecrated Ritual Tools
2. Pyramid shaped stone placed on center of the Altar
3. Frankincense and Myrrh incense, resin or sticks
4. Offering bowl
5. One Red candle
6. Diabetes test lancet/pin/needle
7. Oval piece of parchment with Sigil of Implant Removal on front, the Word of Power **"Eee-AH-Fuh--Huf-Ha-Eee"** spelt phonetically written beneath it, and the following intention statement written on the reverse side-*" It is my Will to remove All Implants from my spirit/body, including the artificial Chakras, once and for all!!"*

Sigil to be used on oval piece of parchment

Eee-AH-Fuh--Huf-Ha-Eee

The Rite Of Chakra Removal step by step

Step One:
Set up all of your Ritual Tools neatly on the Altar. Clear Quartz should be in each corner of your space. Sigil with intention written on it should be placed against the pyramid stone on the center of the Altar so you can clearly see it during the Rite. Have a chair available to sit on during the Rite when called for. Once again you will be burning the oval parchment during the Rite so be prepared by opening a window and have the offering bowl ready. You may light the charcoal you will be using to burn your incense at this point. Now perform the Cleansing Rite Of The Goddess and then light the candles surrounding your space for room lighting. Perhaps one in each direction.

Step Two:
Now cast the Circle Of Heka. Light your incense or place incense on the charcoal. Light the red candle on the Altar.

Step Three:
Gazing at the Sigil on the parchment begin to slowly chant with intention, *"Eee-Ah-Fuh--Huf-Ha-Eee!!"*. Now as you chant, prick your finger and place your blood on the sigil, the intention statement and a drop or two in the offering bowl as well for best results.

Step Four:
Be seated and gaze at the Sigil/parchment leaning against the pyramid stone as you continue to chant. Keep chanting until you are in an altered state. Now stand up, while continuing to chant and burn the parchment using the flame of the red candle. Place it in the offering bowl as it burns.

Step Five:
Now be seated again and begin to meditate on your energy body. Allow the spirits present to guide you in the removal process. Most of the implants will be removed by them at your request, but you need to meditate on each chakra removal one at a time for best results. One by one visualize each Chakra from the Muldahara/Root Chakra to Sahasrara/Crown Chakra being removed. See them being pulled out of your body with all of their constricting energy cords going with them. See them dissolve into ashes before you or you may use what I call a "Portal Of No Return" it is a black hole created with your imagination where you may deposit the implants, returning them to the Universe to be recycled. After the chakras are removed, scan your energy body from feet to head and then repeat scanning your aura chanting the removal word as you do so. If you find large implants, you may focus directly on them as you chant the removal word. Remove them and place them in the Portal Of No Return that you have created.

Step Six:
Now say the following intention statement with authority and finality three times, ***"I am now free of all implants and artificial Chakras!!"***

Step Seven:
Thank all of the Spirits present who have helped with the removal now, and close the Portal Of No Return by seeing it close and vanish in your imagination. Then close the Circle Of Heka and then perform the Cleansing Rite of the Goddess once again.

After the Rite is Finished you may want to do some Chi-Building exercise and fill any spaces that are left open after the removal. Also re-establish your shielding as well or risk being immediately re-implanted.

What to Expect After The Rite

You should notice an immediate increase in your energy levels and psychic abilities. Also less sensitivity to other people's energy junk or less chance of transference of negative energy to you. You will feel all around less anxious and more grounded and centered at all times and this is just the beginning. You will likely feel tired and need to sleep more than usual as well. So be prepared to take it easy for a few days and drink lots of clear, pure water.

You may need to repeat the Implant Removal Rite as needed for maintenance. It is easy to get implanted, and not as easy to realize when it happens. Be alert to your level of spiritual flow and freedom at all times. If you feel an energy drain or a blockage of your energy then you may have been implanted again. If so, relax and talk to spirit if you can, to see if it is the case. If you cannot tell, then you may choose to do the Implant Removal Rite as a precaution. It will not hurt you if you have nothing to remove.

Be alert and keep up with the intention of having no chakras or they will end up growing back or being re-implanted. You can do this by repeating the intention of ***"I am Free of All implants and Artificial Chakras!!"*** daily for a couple weeks time or whenever you feel you should. Also you will need to do a follow up session of meditation/scanning yourself the day after the Rite. The reason is that if you have Controllers (Inter-dimensional beings that keep humanity in drone mode) monitoring you and watching you (because of the occurrence of your awakening) then they will likely try to re-implant you while you are asleep. If this happens to you, stay calm and do a removal meditation within the Circle of Heka as outlined ahead.

Personally I have experienced these Controllers often entering my space at around three-thirty a.m. to re-program me and delete memories etc…for this reason I keep Cursing Words Of Power under my pillow for quick access. I Curse them as soon

I awaken to their presence. You may want to do the same. You will want to do a full cleansing and protection of your Self and Space from all negativity in order to prevent them from entering your space at any time. This particular Rite (called The Rite of Protection) will be provided ahead, in the next chapter.

Implant Removal Meditation

This Meditation may take 15 minutes or it may take an hour, depending on how many implants are left or if you were re-implanted. You may use the Implant Removal Word of Power "Ee-Ah-Fuh--Huf-Ha-Ee" if you choose, but it probably will not be necessary. Also, it you find Archonic Parasites Re-implanted into you then you may want to use either the Cursing Word of Power from Set or the Cursing Word offered by Seker as described in The Rite Of Decimation. The Word from Seker is better for cursing an enemy outside of a ritual setting however. Remember to have the right intention when cursing them...intend to harm them.

Implant Removal Meditation step by step

Step One:
Get comfortable in a seated position and begin to enter a relaxed state by breathing slowly through your nose as if you were going to meditate. Once you are relaxed and are able to use your mind's eye and visualize, begin to scan yourself starting at the top of the head and moving up to your connection to your I.D.S. see a horizontal, flat beam of light scanning slowly upward. Before you start to remove anything, create the Portal Of No Return again. This is a portal that you create with your imagination into which you will send these implants and parasites to a place where they perish or are recycled. This should be about the size of an average window,

and it should look like a black hole sucking up debris that you throw into it.

Step Two:
Here you may find implants along the tube of light above your head connecting to the Higher Self or Inter-Dimensional-Self. Take your time and remove all of these, do not rush and miss any. Take care of the larger ones first (the astral parasites and archon drones). the smaller ones like to hide under layers of energy at the top of the tube of light, all around it. Brush this area with your energy and be prepared for what is released from this area. There may be a legion of implants within this area ready to start falling down into your aura. Create an upside down umbrella like net in your imagination to catch them and close it at the top once they stop falling down. Be very thorough and make sure you get them all. Once they stop falling, brush the layers of energy above your head with your energy hands again and again, and ask Spirit for assistance in getting all of these aura implants to come down. Once they are all in the net, close it and throw it into the black hole that you created.

Step Three:
Now scan down to your head and remove any implants in this area that may be present. Be especially observant of the Upper-Dan-Tien/mind's eye area where most mind control implants are placed. Also, be observant of the back of your head where Archonic parasites usually try to hack your mind. Use your energy hands to throw all of what you find into The Portal Of No Return.

Step Four:
Once all of these are removed, proceed to the upper chest and down to the abdomen removing any implants along these areas.

Step Five:
Now move from your lower abdomen to your legs and feet removing any implants or parasites along this area.

Step Six:
Follow along your grounding cord now and repeat the process.

Step Seven:
Now scan your entire aura and remove any implants that you find here. Make sure that you get your whole aura. If your aura is especially large then take your time and do the work that needs to be done.

That is all for this meditation. Repeat it as needed anytime you feel like you have been implanted again. Check yourself and check with your spirit guides. If you do not have a spirit guide, then a good being to work with in doing this meditation is the Norse God Loki. Call him by chanting his name and then ask for his assistance.

Loki came through for me when I was doing this work for myself and he was a good help along with my spirit guide Mike. Loki looks scary because he is a Daemonic Spirit, but he is not going to hurt you, if anything he will help free you from slavery. Trust him and do what he says in the process of removing your implants.

Chapter 8
The Rite Of Protection

This Chapter will outline a very important Rite of Protection that is necessary during and after you work through this book from this point forward. I recommend that you perform this Rite every other day during this work of Soul Retrieval and as often as necessary after you are done with the book. It will prevent further implantation by the Controllers and other entities who are in league with them. If you are having a lot of trouble with these entities entering your home while you are sleeping, you may want to consider performing the Rite on a daily basis an hour before going to bed.

The Entity that we will be calling upon is one of the Watchers, named Rameel. He is a fallen angel found in the Book of Enoch who has proven to be a potent force of protection in my own life when needed. He will defend you from your enemies and put up wards of protection sufficiently with his balanced Angelic and Demonic power. There is no reason to fear Rameel. All that is needed is respect and to give him gratitude when he does what you ask of him. He usually manifests as reptile like being, but often as a man wearing a hat with glowing electric blue eyes as well.

Rameel has provided me with a word of power that we will use to protect our space in this Rite, as well as words to evoke him into our reality.

Preparation for the Rite

This Rite does not need to be complicated, because is one that we will be performing often. It is important to get comfortable with Rameel and his intense energies first however. In order to do this, I recommend that you take some time to evoke Rameel and perhaps give him a gift of incense (Dragon's Blood is best) with the intention of introducing yourself without asking anything of him. If you are confident that you can handle Rameel's intense energies, then please go ahead and do the Rite without the preliminary evokation. You will need the usual tools with the addition of some Dragon's blood incense if available and also a white sage smudgestick or dried sage leaves. Black candles or candle is to be used for this Rite as well. A white candle may also be appropriate given the cleansing nature of the this Rite.

Checklist of materials
1. Consecrated Ritual Tools
2. Pyramid shaped stone placed on center of the Altar
3. Dragon's Blood incense, resin or sticks
4. Offering bowl
5. One black or white candle
6. Diabetes test lancet/pin/needle
7. Oval piece of parchment with Sigil of Rameel on front, the Word of Power *"Ah-Key-Ohay-Cuh-Eh--He-Huc-Ayoh-Yek-Ah"* spelt phonetically written beneath it, and the following intention statement written on the reverse side-*" It is my Will to Cleanse, Clear and Protect myself and my space/home from all Negativity, Enemies and Harm!!"*

The Sigil of Rameel

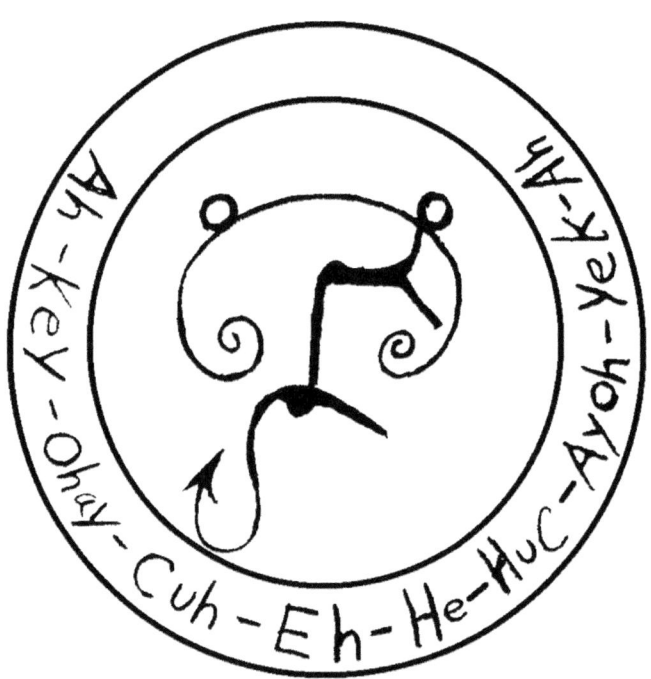

The Rite of Protection step by step

Step One:
Start by setting up your space and Altar as usual with all your tools and the sigil of Rameel as shown above scribed onto a round piece of paper. Lean the Sigil against the Pyramid shaped stone placed on the center of the Altar. Place the black or white candle to the left and slightly in front of the Pyramid or one candle on each side. Offering bowl and bloodletting device should be ready as well. Use Dragon's Blood incense if you have some or another type that is a good quality that puts you in a good state of mind. When you are all set up and ready to begin, you may start by performing the Cleansing Rite of The Goddess now.

Step Two:
Cast the Circle Of Heka, place some incense on the burner or light the stick incense now. Light your candles now as well.

Step Three:
Now prick your finger and place your blood on the Sigil of Rameel, chanting his name as you do so. Be seated and begin to relax as you sing Rameel's Evokation Chant out loud over and over until you feel his presence grow strong:
"Zee-Luh-Ah-Eh-Fee-Ee-Vee-ef--Feh-eev-Ee-Eef-He-Ha-Hul-Eez"
Feel Rameel's presence and then communicate your intention to him as written on the reverse side of his sigil.

Step Four:
When you are ready, begin to chant the Words of Power off of the outer ring of the Rameel's Sigil. Now light your smudge stick or whatever you are using to ward your space (you may use consecrated water instead or in addition). Begin to walk around your space in a circular motion all the while visualizing light coming from you and your smudge smoke and chanting Rameel's protection Words of Power starting at the top left and moving down around the sigil:
"Ah-Key-Ohay-Cuh-Eh--He-Huc-Ayoh-Yek-Ha!!"
See the bright white light cleansing your entire space. Take your time and get every corner of your bedroom and ritual space as well.

Step Five:
When you are done, return to the Altar and take the paper with sigil and intention inscribed on it, fold it up and then burn it in the offering bowl after stating your intention once again. You may, decide to keep the sigil as an open gateway of protective energies and place it in your bedroom while you sleep. This is up to you.

Step Six:
When finished, be sure to thank Rameel and the Neteru and Azazel who held your Magick Circle before ending with the Cleansing Rite of The Goddess.

What to expect after the Rite

You will notice that the area becomes peaceful and stress does not seem as bad. You will find it much easier to sleep in the cleared and protected space without negativity keeping you in a tense state. The Rite is important before bed if you have a lot of negativity being directed at you during this Soul Retrieval work. Remember, when you are sleeping is when you are most vulnerable. If you feel like there are negative entities or energies around, it is important to do this cleansing before going to bed.

Chapter 9
The Rite Of Soul Retrieval

The following Rite should not be taken lightly, nor should it be conducted if the preliminary Rites have not been completed, the Cleansing Rite has not been committed to memory, or if you are still going through heavy changes and clearing from the previous rites.

Please be careful and do not proceed if you are afraid of embracing all parts of your I.D.S. This Rite can cause you to see parts of your own spirit that have been hidden from you your whole life. Now this is for the most part a wonderful thing, but adapting to the new you can be the hard part...or rather trying to be the new you without controversy in your circle of friends and acquaintances in some cases. Another thing that often arises is work or job related...you will have a hard time doing a normal job, unless it is truly what you are meant to be doing.

This Rite causes a shifting in the connection between you and your I.D.S. It makes it ten times stronger and a lot harder to ignore. If you have bad habits that need to be culled, then be prepared to do so before hand. The I.D.S. will insist upon your living your highest good, dreams and even clearing past traumas from your spirit. This can be a hard thing to endure, but it will lead to greater happiness when it is all said and done.

The Neter or Egyptian Underworld God Nehebkau has offered a Word of Power specifically for this Rite and for your Soul Retrieval process. It will be used during the Rite as in earlier Rites.

Results of the Rite may vary depending on the level of your Soul's completeness. If you are already quite happy, healed and complete and you are in alignment with who you truly are, then this Rite may not affect you too much. If you have a wounded, shattered Soul then the opposite will be the case. You will be very empowered and receive tremendous benefit from conducting this Rite.

Preparation For The Rite

For this Rite you will need all the usual Ritual Tools along with the Sigil of Nehebkau which will be provided. And as in other Rites, be prepared mentally for whatever changes and realizations may come. You will need one or two green candles for this Rite. Blue is also acceptable, green or blue being colors sacred to the underworld Gods or specifically Nehebkau. If you are using resin incense then I recommend Copal resin for this Rite. Use an incense that you feel drawn to the most for this Rite though.

You may want to have someone with you through this process as it can be very intense for some, particularly those that are very identified with their gender roles in society and that believe that the most important part of their identity is "male" or "female".

Checklist of materials
1. Consecrated Ritual Tools
2. Pyramid shaped stone placed on center of the Altar
3. Copal resin or incense sticks
4. Offering bowl
5. One or two Green or Blue candles
6. Diabetes test lancet/pin/needle
7. Oval piece of parchment with Sigil of Nehebkau on it, the Word of Power **"ReeHuh-Emuh-Kehfuh"** spelt phonetically, should be written beneath the Sigil. The Intention Statement ***"It is My Will to Magnetize the lost, broken or fragmented parts of my spirit and soul back to me, to be a whole, complete, and powerful being!!"*** must be written on the reverse side of the Parchment.

Sigil of Nehebkau

ReeHuh-Emuh-Kehfuh

Rite Of Soul Retrieval step by step

Step One:
Just as in the Implant Removal Rite, begin by having all your Ritual Tools neatly set up on the Altar, the pyramid stone in the center with the oval parchment and sigil inscribed on it leaning against the pyramid. If you are using two candles, then one on each side of pyramid stone. You may want to lay down at some point during this Rite so that the soul healing can occur more easily. If so, have a yoga mat and pillow at the ready for your use. Light the charcoal for the resin incense now, then perform the Cleansing Rite of the Goddess.

Step Two:
Cast the Circle Of Heka, place some incense on the burner or light the stick incense now. Light the Blue or Green candle/candles now as well.

Step Three:
Gazing upon the Sigil of Nehebkau begin to chant his name and then prick your finger and place your blood on his Sigil and in the offering bowl. You may place some on your intention statement written on the back side of the parchment as well. Now intone his Chant of Evokation a few times to bring him further into your reality: *"Ah-Ree-ah-Cuh-Dee-ef-Kaca-Reed-Dia-Vee-ef--Feh-eev-Aid-Deer-Acak-Feh-Eed-Huc-Ha-Eer-Ha!!"*

Step Four:
Continue to chant *"Neh-Heb-Kau"* and then begin to chant the Word of Power *"ReeHah-Emuh-Kehfuh"* once you feel he is present and in the room with you. Continue to chant *"Neh-Heb-Kau ReeHah-Emuh-Kehfuh"* three more times with your intention in mind. Put your emotions and heart into the intonation. Do not be nervous. You have to mean it for it to work.

Step Five:
Now pick up the parchment and read your intention out loud. Then burn the parchment using the candle flame. Place it in the offering bowl as it burns.

Step Six:
Now lay down, close your eyes and allow the Soul Healing process to take place . Breath through your nose and relax. Long, slow breathing, no thoughts. Just focus on your breath and allow the work to take place. Continue to chant the Word of Power if you feel the need to do so.

Step Seven:
After being still and meditating for about ten to fifteen minutes, come back into a state of alertness, stand up and thank Nehebkau and any other spirits that are present for their assistance in your Soul healing. Now close the Circle Of Heka and then Perform the Cleansing Rite Of The Goddess.

What to expect after the Rite

After you perform this Rite, you may change internally in ways that cause you to feel "different". Specifically, you may feel like you do not fit in with some friends or acquaintances that you use to. This is a normal consequence of Soul Retrieval, but trust me, you are better off without people in your life that are probably not on the same level of spiritual health. They may drag you down if you are overly focused on them. You may feel lonely during transitional periods of time if your usual friends and acquaintances do not understand you anymore. You may even (out of desperation) try to go back to the way you were, but this will not work. I warned earlier that you must be ready for this step as with all the steps in this book, there is no going back to your old self. Abel has been slain…

If you try to forget it all and drop your spiritual work, drop your shielding, and your psychic-defense work then you will just end up a mess, you may even appear to be mentally ill to the uninformed observer. Beware of looking down once you have climbed the ladder to this height. If you keep looking down then you will fall and the impact can be a painful one, which you may never recover from.

One of the reasons that you cannot go back is that your awakening has alerted the forces of mind control that manipulate this world. Once you start to wake up, you will start getting bombarded by them. They are inter-dimensional beings that control this plane from more than one vantage point in space and time, and they will do what they can to bring you down after you start to gain your power back. You must continue to the next chapter to break their influence over you, or eventually get manipulated and fall back asleep. The choice is yours. Trust me, you can do this.

Also, after you do this Rite, the Veil will lift even more so and you will behold the Controllers of this plane holding parts of you captive. This will no doubt cause a feeling of distress, anxiety, and surrealism. You will not know what the hell you are looking at. Just be prepared for some mind-fucks in this process. Not all of you may experience this and some will experience this all the more so. I will explain more later.

After the Rite is completed you will likely also experience traumatic memories returning to you and demanding your attention. Once this happens it is a good idea to talk with either a therapist or a close trustworthy friend who can help you process and heal these past wounds. I found it very helpful to forgive myself over and over for these events in my life where I felt like I had made mistakes and was to blame. I had to forgive myself in order to reintegrate the fragmented soul parts that had returned to me; you will likely experience something similar. Keep in mind the memories that return will often come days or even weeks after you perform the Rite of Soul Retrieval. Stay conscious of your thoughts and feelings during and after the Rite.

Chapter 10
The True Face Of The Moon

This I think, is a touchy subject for many Witches because traditionally we see the Moon as a manifestation of The Goddess. I myself am a Male Witch for sure, but I do not feel the Moon is manifestation of the Goddess energy. Maybe it was at one time, but after years of Magickal Practice in accordance with the phases and influences of the Moon, I have realized that it is no longer what it used to be. The further along that I progressed on my path of awakening and Self-Godhood the more the Moon would send me some harsh and disruptive energies that threw my entire balance off. Then I discovered through information falling into my lap after doing rituals for clarity that the Moon seems to be completely artificial now…it may not have always been this way, but now it is full of machinery and gears. It is a "man" made giant light bulb with what appears to be a space station (like in Star Trek Deep Space Nine) inside of it, except that it is not in space…in fact, space is not what you have been told. The Moon Base, I will call it, is in low orbit and the face of the moon is a light-hologram or perhaps a metal shell covered in dirt. Behind this light-hologram is the "Moon Base" itself. I know this sounds like a science fiction novel, but trust me and go through with the Rites in this chapter and tell me if you do not notice a significant difference in how you think, feel and how your overall psychic energy levels feel. Also, take into consideration that a dusty, rocky surface does not reflect light like a bike reflector…it seems to be it's own light source.

For Witches and those who are reading this that work with Goddess energy I advise you to stop working with the energies of the Moon itself. It is not what it used to be. It is a control center to monitor human thought and human access to their own Inter-Dimensional-Selves. It will not help you, it will only mess with you and confuse you. The true manifestation of the Goddess Energies is the Earth herself and the layer of waters above the Earth known as Gamaliel. Stop being manipulated by the Moon's frequencies. If you are psychic then look for yourself into the moon…see it for yourself. See behind the Veil. If you can see past the illusional energy that the moon is projecting, then you will see the inter-dimensional beings living in this Base looking back at you. They can remote view you the same as you do them, but do not let them scare you. You have much more power than they do.

The inter-dimensional beings look like tall, skinny alien-like humanoids…well they pretend to be aliens, but they are like I said "inter-dimensional beings". Although I am sure aliens do exist, I'm not so sure these qualify as aliens. Not all of these types of beings are working against humans though, keep in mind. There are different tribes of them.

Now another thing to be aware of that is connected to the Moon Base is what I call Sentinel Ships. These ships that look like Star Destroyers in The Star Wars movies and are "V" shaped, uninhabited astral vessels (not physical) that also monitor human thought and frequency. They keep humans locked into their "meat suits" or human bodies. They keep humans from accessing their I.D.S and being the Gods that they are. You will need your cursing weapons at the ready to deal with these in your daily life. Once you begin to pierce the Veils they will probably show up to try to dumb you down and send negative control frequencies to you. Again Sentinel Ships look like Star Destroyers, the major difference being that they are more smooth and metallic looking, not full of bumps and machinery.

Sketch of Moon without holographic face

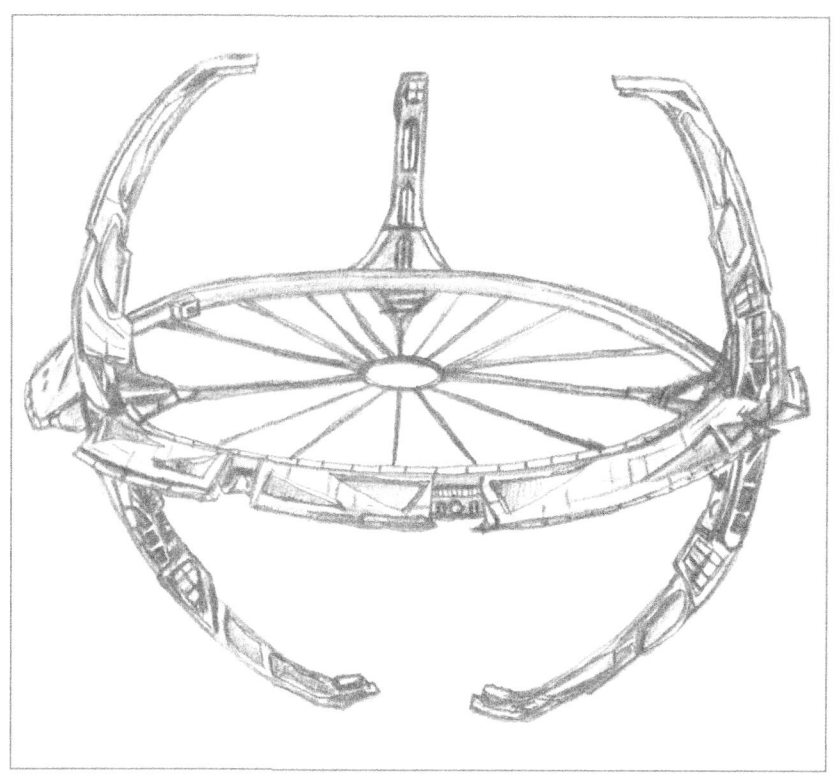

Sketch of Sentinel Ship

The Rite Of Destroying The Artificial Moon's Influence Over You

This Rite will defend your mind and energy from the influence of the Artificial Moon Base. It should be done as soon as possible after the previous Rites. The Rite is a cursing Rite and as before, you have to mean it for it to work right. Do not let the programming instilled into you that tells you that "cursing is wrong" and that "you will have bad karma" scare you out of doing what you need to do to free yourself. These thoughts are mostly conditioning to prevent you from fighting back. The beings who have been controlling you do not have a leg to stand on in terms of "good karma". Thoughts of karma are mostly part of the control system anyway.

The Moon base's inhabitants have been fucking with your energy, your mind, your life and the lives of your loved ones for far too long. It is time to take back your happiness and your power over the false leaders of this Matrix. You are the only leader you need. Get off your knees and curse your enemies!!

The primary frequency used by the Moon are what are called square waves. The primary feeling or thought induced by these control frequencies is guilt. Guilt makes you think you do not deserve to be happy and thus you will accept a miserable, mediocre, slave life. Break the cycle and be the God/Goddess that you are!!

I have successfully performed this cursing Rite and many others without any scary karma backlash bullshit, because I am not doing anything wrong. It is taking back what is yours. You do not have to ask…you take. There is nothing these beings can do once you wake up and dethrone them. Do not let them scare you.

Again, once they realize what you are up to they will try to turn up the fake guilt, fake fear frequencies. Do not buy into it!! It's not real. It's a frequency getting beamed into your body. Keep your shields strong and up at all times during this work to protect your mind and energy. Not only will you feel fake fear and fake doubt, but if you have psychic ability to hear spirit, then you will hear what sounds like your own thoughts saying very fearful and negative things to you. This is a thought frequency getting beamed into your head. I do not care how crazy that sounds because it is what it is. Trust me and do this Rite and feel the difference for yourself. Your access to your I.D.S. will increase all the more, and you will be more of who you are at all times after this Rite.

Preparation For The Rite

For this Rite you will need the Sigils of Ptah, Set and Seker. Set and Seker are the Egyptian Neteru or Gods that have given the Words of Power for cursing and Ptah's Word is for building a charge of energy toward your intention. All Three Sigils are provided ahead along with the curse words for this work of cutting yourself free of mind control. You will need to be prepared mentally for this Rite as well, because of the resistance you may encounter. You will have trouble saying the curse words when the time comes, but you must power through it in a state of sheer Will and drive to break the bonds of the Moon Base's control.

Frankincense and Myrrh resin should be used for this Rite as well. You may want to memorize the curse words for this rite before you begin, so you can intone them clearly without having to read them off a piece of paper. Make sure the lighting is minimal for this Rite. It should be done at night for best results. The moon phase does not matter. Performing this Rite on a full Moon is fine as long as you are prepared for more resistance.

Resistance, like I said will be an increase in feelings of anxiety, fear, doubt about what you are doing. You must ignore these feelings. They will cease the moment your cursing takes effect. The negative frequencies will be unable to affect you. This will give you conviction that what you are doing is the right decision. You must maintain a mental resoluteness throughout this Rite and beyond.

The Moon has no power or control over humans except what we have given it by its matrix of deception. We do Rituals and Magick with the Moon's energy and thus it maintains control over us. Do not participate in moon Rites or Magick after this Rite is complete. If you do, this will only give the Moon power over you once again, and you will have to do the Rite over again.

Definitely be prepared to defend yourself psychically after, before and during this Rite ok. Keep your psychic shielding up at maximum power and use the Curse Breaker Rite as needed at any time you feel like you are being slammed with negative energy. Be aware of how you are feeling…if you feel drained, depressed, sluggish and have no motivation to go on, then perform The Curse Breaker Rite and/or The Rite of Protection as soon as possible.

Checklist of Materials
1. Consecrated Ritual Tools
2. Pyramid shaped stone placed on center of the Altar
3. Frankincense and Myrrh incense, resin or sticks
4. Offering bowl
5. Three Black Candles, one on each side of Pyramid stone, and one behind it.
6. Diabetes test lancet/pin/needle
7. Round shaped parchment with Sigils of Ptah, Set and Seker and the Words of Power spelt as shone on the image below and the following intention written on the reverse side- ***"It is My Will to Harm and Destroy the Moon Base's influence over me, including the Sentinel Ships connected to the Moon Base!!"***
The Front may contain two additional sigils as shown in the image, below the Sigils of the Neteru. These are for additional power towards your intention i.e. to extract/free your energy from the Moon Base's influence.

Sigils to be used on parchment

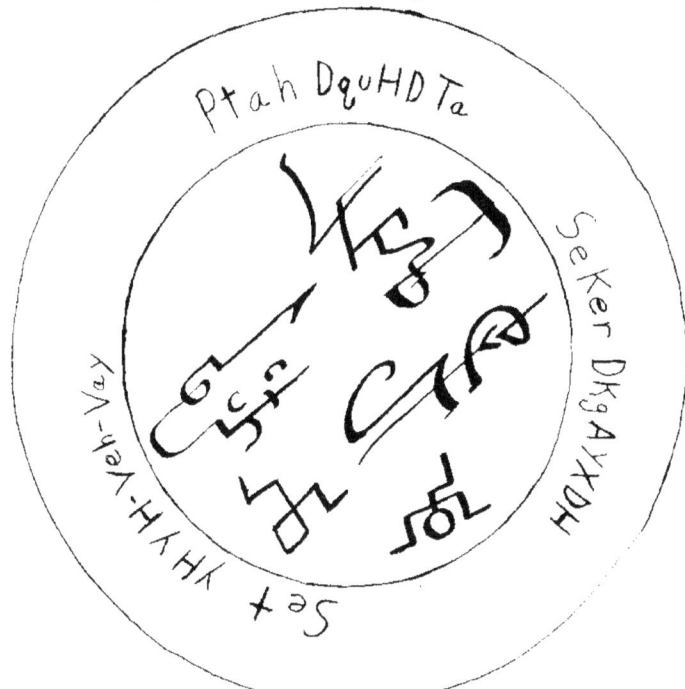

Words of Power to be spoken phonetically in respective order
(clockwise from top)
Ptah-Jeh-kwaoo-Hah-Jeh-Too-Ah
Seker-Jeh-Kuh-Guh-Yeh-Kha-Jeh-Hah
Set-Yuh-Hah-Yah-Hah-Ah-Veh-Vey

The Rite of Destroying The Artificial Moon's Influence Over You step by step

Step One:
Neatly set up all of your Ritual Tools, the pyramid stone, the offering bowl and the three black candles on the Altar. One on each side of the Pyramid stone and one behind the stone. Place the round parchment with sigils on it, leaning against the pyramid stone. Have a chair ready where you can sit comfortably and have the Words of Power you will be using within visual range, just in case you forget them during the Rite. Light the Charcoal for the resin incense now, and perform the Cleansing Rite of The Goddess.

Step Two:
Cast the Circle of Heka and light the three candles. Place some resin incense on the charcoal or light the incense sticks.

Step Three:
Now use your lancet and prick your finger as you begin chanting the names of the Neteru *"Ptah, Seker, Set!!"*. You must evoke them fully during this step. Just chant their names as you drop your blood on their sigils on the center of the round parchment. Make sure there is plenty of incense burning also to aid in their manifestation and then vibrate and sing their Chants of Evokation out loud a few times or until you feel their presence grow strong:
For Ptah:-*"Zee-Reed-Ree-ah-Eh-Dee-Eeoh-Bah-Luh-we-kah-We-Cuh--Huc-Ew-Hak-ew-hul-Hab-Ohee-Eed-He-Ha-Eer-Deer-Eez"*
For Seker-*"Wee-Ree-ah-Dew-Cuh-Eh-Ah-Luh-Dah-Dah--Had-Had-Hul-Ha-He-Huc-Wed-Ha-eer-Eew"*
For Set-*"Dee-eff-Gahee--Ray-Eh-Sah-Ohay---Dew-Vey--Yev-Wed--Ayoh-Has-He-Yar--Eehag-Feh-eed "*

Step Four:
Now be seated facing the Moon, as you cup your hands finger tips to finger tips, thumb to thumb, creating a round container to build a Chi-ball. Begin to chant **"Ptah!!-Jeh-Kwaoo-Hah-Jeh-Too-Ah!!"** Chant this over and over for a few minutes feel your chi building into the orb between your hands. This is raw, powerful energy.

Step Five:
Now chant while focusing on the orb still, **"Seker!! Jeh-Kuh-Guh-Yeh-Kha-Jeh-Hah!!"** over and over. This programs the Chi-ball with a cursing energy. Now do the same with Set's Word of Power **"Set!! Yeh-Hah-Yeh-Hah-Ah-Veh-Vey!!"** His word destroys obstacles. It will program the orb to destroy the obstacle of control (The Moon Base's influence).

Step Six:
Now focusing all your intention on the Moon and Breaking its control over you. Release the Chi-Ball with your exhale and direct it at the Moon Base. Now visualize the Moon exploding like in a Sci-Fi movie. See all the cords and frequency waves directed at you from the Moon, vaporize now. Repeat steps Four to Five and direct another charge to the Sentinel Ships if you feel it is necessary.

Step Seven:
Read your intention on the back of the parchment out loud, then burn it and place it in the offering bowl. Now sit and meditate on the free flowing energy you now have without the suppression-frequencies of the Moon controlling your energy. You may even now access your I.D.S directly and see your body from the outside…relax and let it come. No Barriers. When you are finished, thank all the spirits present one by one. Let them feel how you are grateful. Direct your gratitude toward them.

Step Eight:
Now Close the Circle and Banish your Space with the Cleansing Rite Of The Goddess.

What to expect after the Rite

First thing, do not be fearful of the retaliation that the Moon Base's inhabitants may threaten you with. Remember that they have no power over you. Tell yourself this again and again if they threaten you psychically. You are becoming your own God or Goddess. You do not need them to control you anymore. If necessary the curse words of Set and Seker may be used as needed to keep them at bay. You may even have to repeat the Rite a few times for them to take a hint that you are a free being.

Continue on the path with a resolute mind. There is no turning back now. You are a few more steps away from breaking all the major bonds of the Matrix. You are becoming the only Creator in your life.

Your probably wondering how to do your Magick without thinking of the Moon as an important factor if you are a Witch. I myself have ignored the phases of the moon in my Magick with good results. I suggest that you do the same. Act as if the Moon has no power over you and it becomes your reality. I have done work with the Qliphoth without much trouble entering the sphere that is associated with the Moon known as Gamaliel. This is doable because I do not believe Gamaliel is found within the astral layers of the moon itself, but rather it is an astral realm at the same level as the Moon. The Moon does indicate when the energies of Gamaliel are at their peak (full Moon). I do believe it is an indicator of high energies of Gamaliel, but not the energies of Gamaliel themselves. The Moon seems to harness these energies and use them in a negative way by changing their quality to one of control and the doubt frequency. If you do want to know more about the energies of Gamaliel, I suggest that you evoke and work with Lilith.

Chapter 11
The True Face of Nibiru Exposed

This chapter will deal with this so called "Planet" Nibiru phenomenon. First of all, it is not a planet. It is a Dwarf Star or Sun. It is not very big and it is in actuality a disguised control station in place to monitor Earth's inhabitants. It is not some alien planet here to destroy us or help us. It is a station sending control frequencies to us to dumb us down. That is pretty much all it is. It is inhabited by Inter-Dimensional beings like the Moon Base.

Sorry but aliens are not real in the way that science fiction T.V. and movies teach. Yes there are aliens in terms of beings from other dimensions or realms, but so called "space" is not what you have been taught. Traveling through space will only take you to different time-space states…it is hard to explain, but whether or not you believe it is not important. Let me ask you this; if a rocket pushes to move through outer space and outer space is a void/vacuum with nothing in it? What is the rocket pushing against? How can nothing push something? It can't…

I do however feel that there are aliens in the sense of different or alternate universes. I mean to say that there are other physical planes like this one that are just much different yet still have humanoid inhabitants.

The Rite Of Cursing Nibiru And Destroying It's Influence Over You

What this chapter is about is breaking the influence of Nibiru over your mind and your energy for greater power and access to your I.D.S. I will guide you through the cursing process as with the Moon. It is basically the same Rite and you will be using the same Sigil, but with a different intention statement written on the back of the Sigil. The results are similar. It is the next step on liberating yourself from the forces of mind and frequency control/manipulation.

The Nibiru Base without the cloak, looks similar to the Moon base or station. It is a round disc shaped base with spokes or beams that connect to the center. It sends frequencies that look like spiraling energy…they are disruptive frequencies for whatever reason (I'm not a science expert, but I know what I see in the astral plane). The specific feeling or quality given by this spiral waves is stress. It raises stress levels to an extreme and unnecessary degree. It causes disharmony.

The following Rite must be done as soon as possible after the Moon Cursing Rite. The reason being that once they figure out that you have broken the Moon's influences over yourself, they will likely turn up the intensity of these stress waves, beaming into your head.

Preparation for the Rite

The Rite itself is similar to the Rite of Destroying The Artificial Moon's Influence Over You. The same steps are involved for this Rite, But I will outline them again for you to follow along. Once again, be prepared mentally for an increase in stress and mental discomfort when the energies of this base fight you. You must have a resolute attitude and follow through with conviction and certainty of what you are doing for this Cursing to work. Do not dick around and half-ass this work if you want results.

If you have not already memorized the Curse Words from the previous Rite, now is a good time, if not then have them on hand and in visual range during the Rite.

I do recommend memorizing at least one of the curse words for those pesky Sentinel Ships flying around trying throw you off course with confusion. Just intone the name of Set (or Seker, depending on which curse word you choose) and then the Word of Power itself at any time, any place. You can do it in your head or out loud, depending on your surroundings. Better to do it out loud, if you are alone. I recommend the curse word given by Seker for best-in the moment-results.

While we are on the subject, let me again recommend having a Cursing Word of Power available while you are asleep. Usually around three thirty-three a.m. I find attacks occur on my mind and energy from various different sources. I use the curse words whenever I awaken to an enemy messing with me in some way. Trust me, you want to be prepared for this possibility whether you are a Witch or not.

Be ready as always for retaliation. Have your psychic shielding up and ready at all times during, before and after the Rite. Remember that these beings that you are cursing are psychic and they more than likely know what you are planning by now. Use the Curse Breaker Rite and Word of Power as needed as well.

Checklist of materials

1. Consecrated Ritual Tools
2. Pyramid shaped stone placed on center of the Altar
3. Frankincense and Myrrh incense, resin or sticks
4. Offering bowl
5. Three Black Candles, one on each side of Pyramid stone, and one behind it.
6. Diabetes test lancet/pin/needle
7. Round shaped parchment with Sigils of Ptah, Set and Seker and the Words of Power spelt as shone on the image below and the following intention written on the reverse side- ***"It is my Will to Curse and Destroy the Nibiru Base's influence over me, and to reclaim my Sovereignty & Godhood!!"***
The Front may contain two additional sigils as shown in the image, below the Sigils of the Neteru. These are for additional power towards your intention i.e. to extract/free your energy from the Nibiru Base.

Sigils to be used on parchment

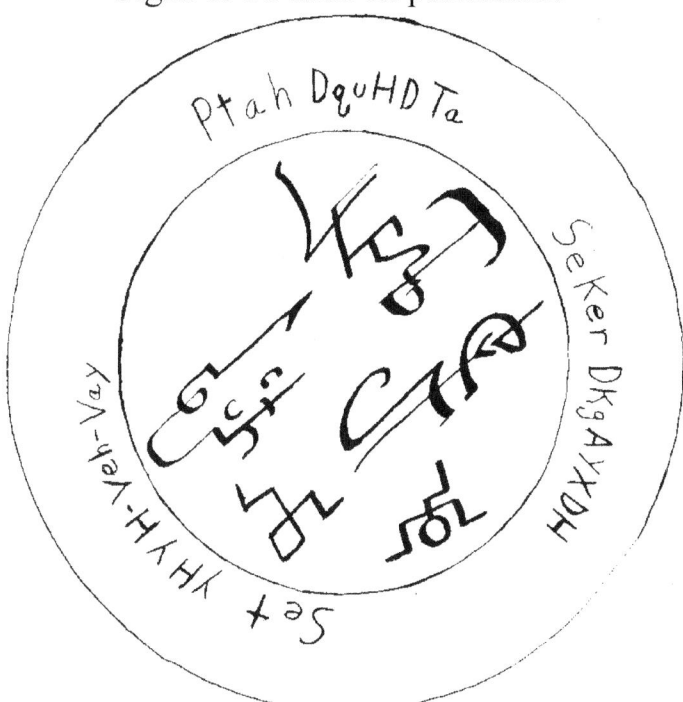

Words of Power to be spoken phonetically in respective order
(clockwise from top)
Ptah-Jeh-kwaoo-Hah-Jeh-Too-Ah
Seker-Jeh-Kuh-Guh-Yeh-Kha-Jeh-Hah
Set-Yuh-Hah-Yah-Hah-Ah-Veh-Vey

The Rite Of Cursing Nibiru And Destroying It's Influence Over You step by step

Step One:
Neatly set up all of your Ritual Tools, the pyramid stone, the offering bowl on the Altar and place the three black candles on the Altar. One on each side of the Pyramid stone and one behind the stone. Lean the Sigil against the Pyramid shaped stone. Have a chair ready where you can sit comfortably and have the Words of Power you will be using within visual range, just in case you forget them during the Rite. Light the Charcoal for the resin incense now and perform the Cleansing Rite of The Goddess.

Step Two:
Cast the Circle of Heka and light the three candles. Place some resin incense on the charcoal or light the incense sticks.

Step Three:
Now use your lancet and prick your finger as you begin chanting the names of the Neteru **"Ptah, Seker, Set!!"**. You must evoke them fully during this step. Just chant their names as you drop your blood on their sigils on the center of the round parchment. Make sure there is plenty of incense burning also to aid in their manifestation. Focus on their Sigils as you chant in order to bring them into your awareness. Sing the Evokation Chants out loud if you can a few times per Spirit:
For Ptah:-*"Zee-Reed-Ree-ah-Eh-Dee-Eeoh-Bah-Luh-we-kah-We-Cuh--Huc-Ew-Hak-ew-hul-Hab-Ohee-Eed-He-Ha-Eer-Deer-Eez"*
For Seker-*"Wee-Ree-ah-Dew-Cuh-Eh-Ah-Luh-Dah-Dah--Had-Had-Hul-Ha-He-Huc-Wed-Ha-eer-Eew"*
For Set-*"Dee-eff-Gahee--Ray-Eh-Sah-Ohay---Dew-Vey--Yev-Wed--Ayoh-Has-He-Yar--Eehag-Feh-eed "*

Step Four:
Now be seated facing the North, as you cup your hands finger tips to finger tips, thumb to thumb, creating a round container to build a Chi-ball. Begin to chant **"Ptah!!-Jeh-Kwaoo-Hah-Jeh-Too-Ah!!"** Chant this over and over for a few minutes feel your chi building into the orb between your hands. This is raw powerful energy. See the energy grow stronger and stronger in intensity.

Step Five:
Now chant the following while focusing on the orb still, **"Seker!! Jeh-Kuh-Guh-Yeh-Kha-Jeh-Hah!!"** over and over. This programs the Chi-ball with a cursing energy. Now do the same with Set's Word of Power **"Set!! Yeh-Hah-Yeh-Hah-Ah-Veh-Vey!!"** his word programs the Chi-Ball to destroy obstacles in your path. It will program the orb to destroy the obstacle of control (The Nibiru Base).

Step Six:
Now focusing all your intention on The Nibiru Base and destroying its control over you. Release the Chi-Ball with your exhale and direct it at the Nibiru Base. Now visualize the Nibiru Base exploding like in a Sci-Fi movie. It looks like a large red star. See all the cords and frequency waves directed at you from the Base, vaporize now. The spiral waves cease and you feel uplifted, relaxed, stress free and well.

Step Seven:
Now Stand up and read your intention on the back of the parchment out loud, then burn it and place it in the offering bowl. Now sit and meditate on the free flowing energy you now have without the stressful, disharmony frequencies of the Nibiru Base controlling your energy. When you are finished, thank all the spirits present one by one. Let them feel how you are grateful. Direct your gratitude toward them.

Step Eight:
Now Close the Circle and Banish your Space with the Cleansing Rite Of The Goddess.

What to expect after the Rite

After you do this Rite. You will notice dramatically less unexplainable stress in your life. You will be more lighthearted and happy. Situations that seemed dramatic stressful before will seem like a nothing like they use to be. You will realize your greater potential and begin to follow the life you always wanted to live. You should notice dramatic improvements in your mood and find it easier to be happy.

Do not stop the work here though. There are a couple more steps and some other things we must explore before you let go of the momentum. If you are overwhelmed by the pace and changes occurring, then I do recommend a short break from the work, but no longer than a week's time. The control forces will try to re-integrate you into their system no doubt. Fight them, keep a positive attitude at all times and do your daily Grounding , Chi-Building, Meditation, and Shielding without giving in to any excuses that are more than likely control forces influencing your thoughts. Stay in alignment with your Inter-Dimensional-Self at all times. Use the Cleansing Rite Of The Goddess daily and as needed.

I also want to share my Soul Retrieval Experience here. By this point in the process of putting the pieces of myself back together, I kept getting glimpses of myself on an operating table with Gray Inter-Dimensional beings starring down at me. The operating table light was shining in my face. This part of my soul was diced to pieces, it was shredded and bloody. It was strapped down…a prisoner of these "Grays"…as they are called. I did not know it was me I was seeing until the after the next Rite was complete. In the days that followed during other Rites of Cursing I saw through the eyes of this part of my soul once again as he was waking up and needed me to free him. I continued on to the next Rite in Chapter 12.

Chapter 12
Frequency Control On The Grid

The grid or the controlled portions of the Earth plane are infused with many controlling devices or programs etc. For example you may have heard of Chemtrails sprayed from military aircraft around earth plane for geoengineering. But geoengineering is only one reason for chemtrails. In actuality it is one of many reason for these toxic gases being sprayed into the atmosphere constantly around the world. The most important reasons that you should be aware of is that these gases make it possible to transmit mind control frequencies more effectively with what are being called "Gwen Towers" or "Death Towers". Other reasons I suspect are to seed the population with various viruses (cold, flu, etc.) and kill off the elderly population as well as causing Alzheimer's disease and other health problems at early ages, also weapon technology that uses the Moon to cause massive storms, earthquakes, tidal waves, you name it…most "natural" disasters are intentional, controlled events. Even the sinking of the Titanic for example I think was intentional. It was capable of sailing off the grid at the time. So they sank it. Think about it, does a piece of ice break through a thick steal wall of a ship that easily. It does not add up in my opinion, seems a little unlikely.

Today we are pretty locked into the Grid so you are better off breaking the control it has rather than leaving it. Leaving the Grid is doable, but it would not be easy to do.

How do I know this? You may ask. It is simple open your mind and break free of the Controllers and you will see reality easily. I am not making these things up. I know it is true. I see reality clearly. I do not have to listen to what others think is reality anymore because I can see for myself. It is very liberating. However in the end, it is only my opinion because I cannot prove these things that I am saying to others. I can suggest that you try the methods in this book and you can see for yourself if you get results or not.

The Death Towers as they have been called, look basically like cell phone signal towers, but are wired with much more than cell phone technology. I am not an expert on specifics of these towers, but I do know that they are a large, important part of the control grid of this Matrix. This knowledge is enough for me to want to destroy their power over myself and my loved ones through effective Magickal Practice means, and that is exactly what we are going to do in this Chapter.

The Death Towers themselves are often hidden on or inside structures and buildings as well. They are in many places hidden from the public.

So basically the Moon Base and the Nibiru Base were heads or control centers, but the Death Towers and chemtrails are still in place and can still effect you unfortunately, but not as much so once you do the following Rite.

Keep in mind though that things like diet and water intake are also controlled here on the Grid. Water is controlled with fluoride and other poisons and also it is targeted by low frequency emitters like the Death Towers. My suggestion is to be careful what you eat and always be thankful for your food. Send your positive energy into your foods and water. If you are attuned to Reiki then Reiki your food and water. If not, you can still clear your food with your connection to your I.D.S. You do not need any attunements to do so.

The Rite Of Destroying Death Tower Control

This Rite is for Cursing the Death Tower's Influence over your mind and your energy. It is one of the last things that I am aware of so far to free yourself before you begin further works of Self Empowerment. Which are in the works at the time of my writing this book. I am excited to bring more knowledge and more power to my readers who want to take all the control back from the false leaders of this Matrix. Spirit is listening to your needs and will deliver I can promise you that.

The Rite is not one that can be directed at a single source but rather at numerous sources of frequencies. For this reason it is done a bit differently than the previous Cursing Rites. It is done once with the intention of breaking you free of the influence of the Death Towers from the point of time that the Rite is performed into the future as well. You will not be using a Chi-Ball for this Rite. You will be employing the help of a powerful Daemoness from the Egyptian Pantheon known as Ammit. She is known as the eater of souls...and ironically she will help you reclaim the lost fragments of your soul.

Preparation for the Rite

For this Rite you will need one to three black candles, a chair to sit in when needed during the Rite, The Sigil of Ammit with the unbinding Sigils below her's. Both will be provided ahead. Use all the usual Ritual Tools and the offering bowl. Incense is recommended, but Ammit is not concerned with which incense you burn, as long as it something that works for you. More important than incense for this rite is several good drops of blood dedicated to Ammit for her service and to show her your respect. Be warned she is not a force to be arrogant with or disrespect in any way.

For this Rite Ammit has provided a Word of Power to intone that is used to unleash her destructive force on your targets . It is the only Word you will be using in the following cursing process.

If you have not yet had a part of your soul return to you, then be prepared for the occurrence of such at the conclusion of this Rite. You may want to memorize or have within visual range the soul retrieval Word of Power given by Nehebkau just in case you need it to magnetize any soul fragments that may potentially be released during or after the Cursing. The Word spelt phonetically is ***"ReeHuh-Emuh-Khefuh".*** Remember to say the Name of Nehebkau then the Word of Power for a stronger effect.

Also be prepared for retaliation and curses being directed at you. Have your psychic shielding up and strong before, after and during the Rite. Use the Curse Breaker Rite and Atum's Word of Power as needed.

Checklist of materials

1. Consecrated Ritual Tools
2. Pyramid shaped stone placed on center of the Altar
3. Your choice of incense, resin or sticks
4. Offering bowl
5. One to three Black Candles, one on each side of Pyramid stone, and one behind it.
6. Diabetes test lancet/pin/needle
7. Round shaped parchment with both the name and Sigil of Ammit, the unbinding Sigil below hers and the Word of Power *"Yee-Zee-Me--Eem-Eez-Eey"* written on the front. The following intention must be written on the reverse side *"It is my Will to Destroy the controlling influences of the Death Towers over me!! By the Power of Ammit and of my I.D.S.!! My Will be done!!"*

Sigil to be used

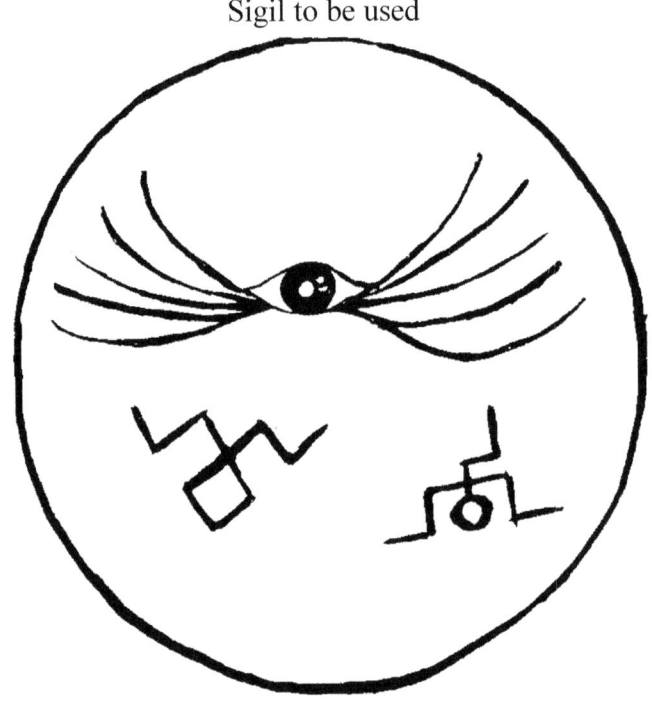

Ammit
Yee-Zee-Mee--Eem-Eez-Eey

The Rite Of Destroying Death Tower Control step by step

Step One:
Neatly set up all of your Ritual Tools, the pyramid stone, the offering bowl on the Altar and place the three black candles on the Altar. One on each side of the Pyramid stone, and one behind the stone. Place the round parchment with sigil on it, up against pyramid stone. Have a chair ready where you can sit comfortably and have the Word of Power you will be using, within visual range. Just in case you forget it during the Rite. Light the Charcoal for the resin incense now, light any candle in the room for lighting and perform the Cleansing Rite of The Goddess.

Step Two:
Cast the Circle of Heka, light the black candle/candles on the Altar and place some incense on the charcoal or light the stick incense.

Step Three:
Now as you chant the name "Ammit" over and over, prick your finger and place a few generous drops of blood on the her Sigil and place another drop or two in the offering bowl as well.

Step Four:
Now be seated, facing the North and the Altar as you gaze upon the parchment with her Sigil on it continue chanting her name until you feel her presence in the room with you. Now intone her Chant of Evokation out loud over and over until you feel her presence with you fully:
"Cuh-Eh-Dee-OoAy-Dew-Fee-Vey-Jee-Dee-ef-Eh--He-Feh-eed-Eej-Yev-Eef-Wed-Ayoo-Eed-He-Huc!!"

Step Five:
Now begin to chant *"Ammit Yee-Zee-Mee--Eem-Eez-Eeyeh!!"* thinking of your intention as you intone the Word or Power over and over until you feel your Will is received by the Universe and Ammit.

Stand and take the parchment into your hand and read the intention on the reverse side out loud, then light it on fire with the black candle on the Altar. Now place it in the offering bowl as it burns. Feel the intention being received by the Universe and Ammit as the smoke rises.

Step Six:
Now be seated and meditate on your gratitude for your freedom from Death Tower Control and frequency control. Use the Word of Power from Nehebkau to draw any fragments of your soul that may have been released during the Rite. Say *"Neh-Heb-Kau ReeHah-Emuh-Kehfuh"* out loud with intention, Will and emotion.

Step Seven:
Now express gratitude to the spirits present one by one and close the Circle. Then Use the Cleansing Rite Of The Goddess.

What to expect after the Rite

Again as in previous Cursing and Soul-Retrieval Rites in this book, be aware of your feelings and any images of soul fragments that come to mind. Draw these fragments back to yourself when you see them. Usually you will see through the eyes of the Soul fragment. So just pay attention to what your mind's eye sees after the Rite.

You may need to use the Cursing Words of Power again in order to free them fully from the Controllers. If you have not seen them already they look like tall, gray "aliens" or what is passed off as an alien in the deception agenda. Remember they are not aliens, they are inter-dimensional beings.

You may need to repeat some of the Cursing Rites we did in this book as needed and also implant removal may need to be repeated as needed as well. When repeating the cursing Rites you may now ask Ammit or even Rameel to curse your Spirit Enemies for you as needed. They are powerful cursers and can keep you protected and free from your enemies daily if need be.

Chapter 13
What Comes Next?

With the completion of the Soul Retrieval Work in its entirety behind you, you are now free to pursue other initiatory work and systems of Magickal practice and receive the full benefit from the Magick you perform. There are no more barriers between you and your I.D.S. The most important work of the Left-Hand-Path starts here.

You must however maintain Energy Management practices indefinitely if you want the work you have done to last, and you may need to repeat some of the Rites in this book as needed.

Another important part of this work to maintain your physical health also. You must keep your physical vehicle healthy or you will face health problems like anyone else. Maintaining your physical health creates a good amount of healthy Chi energies in the body, but remember it is a balance and exercising too much will blowout your Chi.

The work you have completed in this book was the first step on the ladder of ascension from a Left-Hand-Path perspective. If you move into other Left-Hand-Path works then I recommend books that teach how to ascend as your own God. Continue on the path of becoming sovereign; becoming your own leader. Do not go backwards and let others tell you what to believe. Do not bow down to false leaders like a sheep, seriously stop buying into this fake system of control.

I never once in my entire life voted. Why? You may ask, the reason is that I always knew deep down, even when I was a young child that the government was a lie…it is a system created to give the illusion of choice to the drone race known as humans. I know that may make you angry to hear me say that. I am not a fake leader…I am right here with you. I suffered at the hands of the false leaders and this Matrix in ways that you may never know, nor do I wish it upon you. I am here with you. I know your frustration and suffering with the intentionally confusing and manipulative political system of most of this plane. I say most because there are a few places left in this plane that have not been bombed by America or it's allies for not playing ball with them. The so called "elites" want to destroy us, but at the same time they need us because they have no power of their own. We are all in this fish tank together.

As I said before, I am not making this stuff up. I am a gifted psychic and after years of empowering practice and overcoming the programming and the lies of this Matrix. I have accepted reality for what it is…illusion. It is an illusion which we may eventually possess full control over and make our true desires a reality. This plane will be a much better place if you will all awaken to your reality and stop buying in to the false leader's lies.

The governments of this world answer to the Controllers. Which means no matter who you vote into office you will have the exact same results as far as what is done…the result is the following. YOU ARE A SLAVE!!!! You work your ass off and then pay all the money you earned into survival with little left to enjoy your life and then you still end up in debt…have any of you noticed that you are slowly having to work more and more and still you become poorer and poorer. This is even more true for people who do regular nine to five jobs…they literally work themselves into a grave and they are still in debt when they die…but I digress. They believe in the retirement idea, like life will be better when they retire. In most cases people are too old to really enjoy life anymore by the time they can fully retire. This is why it is important to do what we really love in life. To make our dreams a reality.

What I am trying to say is, I want you to take the initiative and create what you really want for yourself. Do not settle for slavery. If you have sincerely done the Rites in this book then you will not be able to be a slave drone any longer. You are a leader now!! You are a God or Goddess in the flesh!!

Afterword

Thank you for taking the time to read through and practice the techniques in this book. I hope they work for you and free you from the shackles of the Matrix the way they have I and my sister, Sara. Please take the time to write me some feedback and allow me to answer any of your questions about this work that you may have.

You can find me on You-Tube. Just search Enoch Petrucelly to find my channel or visit my Facebook Page *Enoch Sigil Creator And Card Reader* to message me directly.

Check out my other books on Amazon.com. Type in my name to find my author page.

Again, Thank you and may the Goddess be with you always!

Enoch B. Petrucelly
LHP Male Witch
April 28th 2018

Printed in Great Britain
by Amazon